I0759477

CONSIDER THE LILIES

365 DEVOTIONS FOR WOMEN

BroadStreet
PUBLISHING

BroadStreet Publishing Group, LLC.
Savage, Minnesota, USA
Broadstreetpublishing.com

CONSIDER THE LILIES

9781424570836
9781424570843 (eBook)

Typesetting and design by Garborg Design Works | garborgdesign.com

Compiled and edited by Michelle Winger | literallyprecise.com

Printed in China.

25 26 27 28 29 30 31 7 6 5 4 3 2 1

Consider the lilies, how they grow:
they neither toil nor spin,
yet I tell you, even Solomon in all his glory
was not arrayed like one of these.

Luke 12:27 ESV

INTRODUCTION

Discover the peace that comes from trusting in God's faithful care, provision, and protection. This devotional book invites you to let go of worry and embrace a life anchored in God's promises.

Consider the Lilies will encourage you each day to release your anxieties and find comfort in God's unchanging love. Through daily reflections, Scriptures, and prayers, you'll be reminded that God still provides for the lilies and watches over you with even greater care. Experience a year of hope, peace, and trust in God's faithful provision.

Be assured that you are held by a loving Father who meets every need and rest in the knowledge that his protection surrounds you wherever you go.

JANUARY

Jesus Christ is the same
yesterday and today and forever.

Hebrews 13:8 NASB

PROVISION

May He who supplies seed to the sower, and bread for food, supply and multiply the seed you have sown and increase the fruits of your righteousness.

2 Corinthians 9:10 NKJV

The beginning of generosity is provision. Just as a farmer requires seed for a harvest, we must also be provided with something to sow. God has supplied you with everything you need to help grow his kingdom. He will increase your resources as you diligently plant the seeds of faith.

As God multiplies your resources, he will also increase the harvest; that is, the good that comes from what you have sown. He gives to you generously that you might be generous.

Be encouraged to give from what he has given you and watch the blessings in your life increase.

BRISK WALK DEEP TALK

Bodily exercise profits a little, but godliness is profitable for all things, having promise of the life that now is and of that which is to come.

1 Timothy 4:8 NKJV

There's nothing like a brisk walk to get your heart rate up and help you to clear your head. If you are headed outside, it can be a time to cut yourself off from all the distractions that easily grab you when you are home. You might be someone who likes to put something in your ears when you exercise—like music or inspirational messages.

Try something different the next time you head out. As this Scripture says, the exercise does benefit you but so will a great conversation with a close friend.

Combine exercise with time to connect with someone you love. Listen, talk, and encourage one another in your faith.

GET TOGETHER

When we get together, I want to encourage you in your faith, but I also want to be encouraged by yours.

ROMANS 1:12 NLT

There is something wonderful about meeting up for coffee or a quick dessert. Not only is this a simple pleasure, but it sets the tone for good conversation. You probably have a lot of conversations throughout your day, but it is good to be intentional with those in your life who help to build you up in your faith.

Take some time to get together with another believer and share with them what God has been teaching you right now. Ask them questions. Take advantage of times together to encourage each other and wrestle with some bigger questions of faith.

Invite Jesus into your time with friends and watch the growth in your lives as you experience the joy of getting together.

PRESENCE

You will show me the way of life,
granting me the joy of your presence
and the pleasures of living with you forever.

Psalm 16:11 NLT

It doesn't always feel like life is full of God's presence and pleasures. Sometimes it actually feels like the opposite. Many of the psalms explore the feelings of those times when God feels absent, and it's important to acknowledge these as genuine human emotions.

The truth is that God is always near and willing to show us the way of life. Sometimes our darkest times can turn into our closest times with our maker.

If you are feeling estranged from him right now, ask him to grant you the joy of his presence and allow your heart to be filled with the knowledge of living into eternity.

TAKE NO OFFENSE

People who aren't spiritual can't receive these truths from God's Spirit. It all sounds foolish to them and they can't understand it, for only those who are spiritual can understand what the Spirit means.

1 Corinthians 2:14 NLT

It can be easy to have a day full of wondering where God is in the middle of it all. We can admit that sometimes faith in Christ seems absurd. We can feel a form of persecution when we hear others laugh about Christianity or find a way to blame religion for all the wrong in the world.

To the world, the message of the cross is offensive. To those of us who believe, however, we find in the message of Christ our true fulfilment because it is a message full of hope, peace, and joy. Jesus can handle your doubt but ask him to restore an unwavering faith so you know you are living in the truth.

Choose not to be offended by someone's ignorance of your faith today. Pray for them instead.

BREATH OF GOD

The earth was without form and void, and darkness was over the face of the deep. And the Spirit of God was hovering over the face of the waters.

GENESIS 1:2 ESV

You might not consider yourself very spiritual if you benchmarked yourself against how often you pray, attend church, or read the Bible. However, as a believer, you have received Jesus who has breathed new life in you.

The word for the Holy Spirit in this verse, *ruach*, can mean wind, breath, or spirit. The Spirit that was hovering over the waters in the beginning is the same Spirit that lives in you and is as natural as your breathing.

You don't have to be religious or have nailed down every spiritual discipline, just be welcoming of the Holy Spirit within and watch him turn the ordinary into something extraordinary!

STILL HOPE

"Now, O Lord, for what do I wait?
My hope is in you."
Psalm 39:7 ESV

In the innocence of our youth, it can be so easy to believe things that seem impossible. The opportunities of life are like an open book before us. When our stories are in the beginning stages, there is an ease and rhythm to everything. The thought of the future is exciting to most, not intimidating. The more life we live, the more experience we get, and the more unknown variables insert themselves into our stories. What once seemed simplistic is complicated by matters that challenge our belief systems.

But this is where our stories deepen, and the faithfulness of the Lord shines through the testing of our faith. Through it all, God is unchanging. His loyal love never leaves us. As our understanding of his kindness deepens along with the pain we inevitably experience, our capacity for extending his mercy also grows.

Continue to hope, for there is always more available through fellowship with the Spirit.

CONTINUAL SURRENDER

By the help of your God, return;
Observe mercy and justice,
And wait on your God continually.

HOSEA 12:6 NKJV

It is never too late to build a life on the foundation of God's mercy. Whether you have been following him for decades or for days, each moment is a new opportunity to rely on his love. His ways are better than our own. His wisdom is purer than the logic of the world's systems. God is more reliable than the sunrise.

When we learn to wait on him, we are better for it. Instead of rushing ahead in our own strength to accomplish what we think is best, let us surrender our plans to him. As we move forward, when we know him well, we will know when to pause, when to redirect, and when to keep pushing through.

Above all, know him well. Love him well, being merciful and promoting justice and peace with your life. You will not be disappointed when he is your constant help and guide.

A WAY PREPARED

"Build up, build up, prepare the road!
Remove the obstacles out of the way of my people."

ISAIAH 57:14 NIV

There is an open road to heaven's gates laid out before us. The courts of our great God and King are welcoming and accessible to all who will enter in. Jesus made it clear through his life and through the ministry of his Word that all who want to come to the Father must come to him first.

Through Jesus, we are able to enter into unhindered connection with the Father of glory. There are no hoops to jump through, no moving targets to master in order to know God.

In submission to God, through faith in Jesus, and in the aligning of your life with his loyal love, you will find yourself at home in him with no obstacles to separate you.

IN THE MEANTIME

It is not yet time for the message to come true,
but that time is coming soon; the message will come true.
It may seem like a long time, but be patient and wait for it,
because it will surely come; it will not be delayed.

HABAKKUK 3:2 NCV

When we are waiting on the fulfillment of God's promises in our lives, and in the world at large, it is important to maintain the right perspective. God's timing is not our own. Where we would be hasty, God is full of patience, waiting for all things to be properly aligned in his purposes. He is not slow in answering his promises.

God is full of mercy, and he can see what we cannot. He is faithful. His character is unchanging. Instead of being influenced by our circumstances, let's let our faith influence them. God's truth will always prevail, and he will not be made a liar.

Practice patience and persistence. He is making a way, and when he says it is time, nothing will stop him.

AN EXCELLENT FIGHT

I have fought an excellent fight. I have finished my full course with all my might and I've kept my heart full of faith.

2 Timothy 4:7 TPT

When you are training, it is one thing to persevere in preparation. Some days you may hit your mark, and others you may struggle to meet it. But there is nothing like the energy and thrill of a crowd to push you beyond your normal peak. Knowing that others are watching can cause one to gain a new burst of energy and focus.

In faith, too, there are times when we are pushing through with all we've got on the lonely stretches. But then we remember that there is a crowd of witnesses cheering us on. Let us throw off the things that hinder us and keep that pace. The finish line is not far off!

There is strength to be found in the camaraderie of faithful followers in the race of life. Remember today that you are not doing this alone.

WELCOMED IN

"Everything that the Father gives Me will come to Me, and the one who comes to Me I certainly will not cast out."

John 6:37 NASB

We have been welcomed in with open arms into God's great kingdom through Jesus. We come to him through faith, and he transforms us by the power of his Spirit in our lives. He will never turn us away when we come to him.

Let that sink in. He welcomes you with the undying affection of a father toward his children. He runs to meet you whenever you turn to him. There is nothing that could keep him from meeting you. His love compels him toward you, so run freely toward him without delay.

Whatever your hesitations have been, leave them behind today and run into the arms of your loving God. He is already running toward you.

NO DOUBT

Let him ask in faith, with no doubting, for he who doubts is like a wave of the sea driven and tossed by the wind.

JAMES 1:6 NKJV

There is nothing on earth that compares to the life God has called us to and wants to bless us with. When we are able to overcome our doubt and live by faith, we will experience a freedom which is not available any other way. Yet we all, admittedly, struggle with doubts.

There is no hope for us unless we anchor ourselves in the Word of God and ask him to hold us with his mighty hand. In his grasp, we will be safe from the crashing waves of life that attempt to drown us and pull us under. Peter stepped out of the boat in faith and began to sink because of doubt, so Jesus reached out and saved him in his mercy.

You don't ever need to doubt God, but when you do, he will still keep you from drowning because of his abundant mercy and love for you.

MOVING MOUNTAINS

Every valley shall be raised up,
every mountain and hill made low;
the rough ground shall become level,
the rugged places a plain.

ISAIAH 40:4 NIV

There is no way out. Ever feel that way? Life can present us with ways that seem like dead ends, capable of opening up only if there is some type of supernatural intervention. We confess we need a miracle.

Thankfully, we have a miracle worker, and he is always working on our behalf in unseen places. He sees everything that we are going through. He is capable of moving our mountains, parting our seas, and eventually, bringing us into eternity, where he has prepared a place for us. Nothing is impossible with our God.

When you hit a wall and there appears to be no solution, remember that you serve a God of limitless power. Go to him in faith and expectation of what he will do.

HE HAS DELIVERED

When the righteous cry for help, the Lord hears
and delivers them out of all their troubles.

Psalm 34:17 ESV

We have been told that there are no guarantees in life, but for the children of God, there are. We have a promise from God that when we, who have been made righteous by the blood of Christ, call out to him, he hears, he answers, and he delivers. That is the absolute truth.

God's ways are higher than ours. When we cry out to him, we sometimes think we have the perfect and only solution. But then God overrules, and we should be thankful that he does. He gives us his very best, delivering us in his wisdom and love.

Call out to God today and listen to his solution for your troubles. He knows you better than anyone in all of time and space, and he will move toward you in love and faithfulness.

SINKING SAND

He lifted me out of the pit of despair,
out of the mud and the mire.
He set my feet on solid ground
and steadied me as I walked along.

Psalm 40:2 NLT

When you were a little kid, did you ever play sinking sand? It is a game that usually involves jumping from pillow to pillow or couch to couch because if you touch the ground, that's sinking sand! As adults we can fall into the routine of living life the same way, jumping from one thing to the next, terrified of failure. Life in Christ doesn't need to be like this though.

No good pursuit or busy schedule is going to save you. A life built on the solid foundation of Jesus Christ is the only thing that will keep you grounded. He is the solid ground, steady and sure, and even if you fail, you can never mess up enough to sink.

Be aware of your footing and what you trust in today and pray about if you need to shift to relying on Christ instead of other things.

ALWAYS GOOD

The LORD is good to those whose hope is in him,
to the one who seeks him.

LAMENTATIONS 3:25 NIV

You know how you can hear about a restaurant and how great a particular dish is from others, but it's not until you taste it for yourself that you really know? You have to experience it firsthand to be able to proclaim to someone how good it is. You run a risk when you go partake of the meal, however. You risk it not being as good as you hoped; you risk being let down.

There is a risk when we hope. When we choose to partake of hope, we risk being let down by whatever it is we are hoping in or for. Is God really as good as everyone else has said he is? As the Scriptures proclaim he is? The only way to really know is to hope in him—to take a risk and find out.

Here's a little secret: God never disappoints. He is good, but don't settle for taking everyone's word on it! Taste and see, and find out for yourself.

NEW SELF

Put off your old self, which belongs to your former manner of life and is corrupt through deceitful desires, and to be renewed in the spirit of your minds, and to put on the new self, created after the likeness of God in true righteousness and holiness.

EPHESIANS 4:22-24 ESV

Paul makes a distinction between life before Christ and life after. He is not asking us to simply replace sinful lifestyle with a moral lifestyle or obviously bad deeds for seemingly good deeds. He is telling us that when we become Christians, we are handed a new life in Christ. A difference should be present.

In verse 17, Paul talks about life before Christ and how people have futile minds. This means they are living with no regard for God or his ways. They are self-focused and living with no thought to eternal consequence. He mentions that this is a thought pattern.

Do you live as if God exists? Put off your old self and walk in freedom and life with God.

PROMISED INHERITANCE

Your faith and love rise within you as you access all the treasures of your inheritance stored up in the heavenly realm. For the revelation of the true gospel is as real today as the day you first heard of our glorious hope, now that you have believed in the truth of the gospel.

COLOSSIANS 1:5 TPT

The promises of God are a guarantee; they aren't going anywhere. Your inheritance is a sure thing. Believing in Jesus is not a bait-and-switch tactic or a gimmick with a catch. When you choose to follow him, Jesus says that his promises toward you are a done deal. And who is more faithful than God? His reputation of keeping his promises and being faithful proceed him. This is a truth that cannot be shaken or stolen and doesn't get destroyed or old and broken with time.

The glorious truth of trusting in Jesus is just as wonderful on day 1,000 as it is on day one. Isn't that good news? Let this news bring you hope. Let your faith and love rise up in your soul as you consider the sure foundation that you stand on.

Don't let the gospel message become old or stale. Open your mouth in praise to the Creator and in exclamation of this truth to those around you.

NEVER LACK

The LORD is my shepherd,
I have what I need.
He lets me lie down in green pastures;
he leads me beside quiet waters.

PSALM 23:1-2 CSB

The world wants to tell you that what is most important is taking care of yourself. It says that your self-care is all up to you, and to feel better in life you just need to get away, get a manicure, get a massage, or take a trip to the mall. Though these things are not bad, they fall short, as most of our attempts at self-care will.

Instead, look to God to supply all your needs. Turning to your good shepherd is the best self-care gift you can give yourself; it's the only one that will truly heal and refresh. Jesus is waiting to whisper to you, "In me, you will never lack."

There is only one who can bring you to waters that will make you never thirst again and bread that will alleviate all hunger. Only one can restore your soul—Jesus.

SOUL RESTORATION

He restores my soul;
He leads me in the paths of righteousness
For His name's sake.

Psalm 23:3 NKJV

You've already chosen to let God care for you by picking up this book. It shows that you place a priority on reading his Word. Good job! There are many important things asking for attention but being in his Word and in prayer are the most important for your faith. Continue to persevere in this, dwelling in his Word and praying.

Instead of hitting snooze in the morning, grab that cup of coffee and your Bible. Sleep is important, but Jesus is better than that extra fifteen minutes every time. It can be hard to ask for help, but those who find God as their happy place embrace dependency on God.

Asking God for what you need is the action that shows the posture of your heart. You want the posture of your heart to be turned toward the Father. He alone will restore you.

EVERY DAY REFRESHMENT

Fill us with your love every morning.
Then we will sing and rejoice all our lives.

Psalm 90:14 NCV

Many of us take time to start our mornings with a full mug of coffee or tea. Reading this devotional means you're also taking time to fill your soul. What is the key to a good life? It's this right here—being filled with God's love. Just like our morning beverages, we need it fresh every day. Most of us empty our coffee mugs every morning and our spiritual mugs every day.

If you are living a life for God, you are constantly pouring into those around you, which is a great thing! But those who pour out need to be filled up again. When you start your days in your strength and skip out on God's Word, you start on empty. Most people don't like cold, old coffee either. If you set your mug down and forget about it, do you pick it up a few days later and drink it? Usually not. When the coffee gets cold and old, it usually gets thrown out.

Bring your cold heart before the flame of God every day and ask him to fill it afresh.

CONTENT IN CHRIST

I know what it is to be in need, and I know what it is to have plenty. I have learned the secret of being content in any and every situation, whether well fed or hungry, whether living in plenty or in want.

Philippians 4:12 NIV

Self-help book after self-help book promise you the secret to the life you've always wanted. They keep getting published. If you just pay a small fee, or use this product, or join our program, we promise it will change your life! You've heard it before. They can be rather alluring, don't you think? Who doesn't want to be in on a grand secret that can make life better? But none of those man-made methods will satisfy.

Paul writes the secret right here: a timeless truth that trumps them all. Do you want to know the secret to contentment? You find it in Christ. That's the secret. If you are abiding in Christ, you can live content in poverty and in wealth. You can live content through trials and in joyous moments. You can be satisfied in any circumstance because your rock and refuge are Christ. It's not a trick, not a gimmick, not a "but wait, there's more!" kind of ad.

It's really this simple: abide in Christ and God will give you everything you need.

KEEPING PACE

Fight the good fight of faith; take hold of the eternal life to which you were called, and for which you made the good confession in the presence of many witnesses.

1 Timothy 6:12 NASB

Do you admire people who are really into running? Maybe you are an avid runner. There is a lot to be learned from the sport of running that can be used as a metaphor for the Christian life. The apostle Paul likens our Christian life to a race, not because we are competing against one another, but because to run a long race it takes endurance.

Endurance is an important character trait that you grow in as you allow the Holy Spirit to do his sanctifying work in you. There is a shift in your life when you realize that being a Christian is not just a prayer you pray, but a lifetime race that requires you to keep pace with the Holy Spirit.

God is not a crazy task master; he's the perfect coach, gently working with you to become more like Christ.

DRAWING CLOSER

The Lord is near to all who call on him,
yes, to all who call on him in truth.

Psalm 145:18 NLT

If things don't turn out the way we have planned, does that mean that God hasn't answered our prayers? We can't simplify our life and prayers and God like that. When we do, we put God in a box—where he does not belong. God is not our great genie in the sky, granting wishes or denying them.

A red flag in this area would be if you move on and forget about God when he answers your prayer until the next time a request pops up. Prayer is a part of your relationship with God. It strengthens your faith, exposes your weaknesses, and leads to real communion with the Father. God won't always answer your prayers the way you think he should or even in the time that you want.

Do you see a red flag in your prayer life? Come to God with expectancy to grow in a relationship instead of demanding your own way.

GROW UP

When I was a child, I spoke and thought and reasoned as a child. But when I grew up, I put away childish things.

1 Corinthians 13:11 NLT

The writer of Hebrews is not saying that simple teachings, like repentance and faith, need to be abolished in the church. There is nothing new under the sun; no new revelation is going to come down. The writer is making a case for believers to strengthen what they know about these matters, and then continue learning Scripture.

Sometimes, we can mistake new enlightenment with maturity. There is the temptation to create something new out of Scripture, to find a new way or a new revelation and follow it. This makes people appear mature and knowledgeable about the Bible. Though we are called to grow and mature, be wary of teachings that offer something new.

Scripture is alive, and it doesn't need to be reborn. Become mature in the wise teachings of Scripture and grow in your faith.

INVITATION TO SURRENDER

"You of little faith, why are you so afraid?"
Then he got up and rebuked the winds and the waves,
and it was completely calm.

MATTHEW 8:26 NIV

Life is not a steady stream. It comes at us in waves. Waves of achievement, of grief, of joy, of pain. Just like waves sweep in and out of the ocean, life ebbs and flows around us. Life is like the waves that crashed up against the rocking boat where the disciples sat.

You have an invitation this morning to surrender your boat. You can step out of whatever earthly thing your security is in as you navigate the waves coming at you. You can step out in faith in the one who can calm those waves.

As you come out of your boat, look into the eyes of Jesus. Those who step out of their boats keep their eyes focused on Jesus, not on the waves around them.

STICK WITH IT

Patient endurance is what you need now,
so that you will continue to do God's will.
Then you will receive all that he has promised.

Hebrews 10:36 NLT

Before GPS and smart phones, people had to use atlases. They would keep these big paper maps in their cars. When they went on a road trip, they pulled out the map, using highlighters to mark out the route. Now, technology maps it out for us, warning us about roadblocks, construction, and even hazards ahead. What luxury!

In this journey of faith, we all experience trials and tribulations. Like a GPS, James is warning us that there will be hazards and roadblocks ahead. The destination? Spiritual maturity. Going through tough things doesn't mean you've strayed onto a backroad, leaving God's mapped out plan for your life. Though sin can do that to us, we often face the very trials God has placed for us to persevere through on these supposed backroads.

Trials will build your faith and make you more mature in Christ, helping you get to your final destination. Take heart and be blessed as you persevere.

WALKING

What you have heard from the beginning is to remain in you. If what you have heard from the beginning remains in you, then you will remain in the Son and in the Father.

1 John 2:24 CSB

Doctors will tell you it's important to stay active. Even a simple walk around the block is good for your health. We don't walk as much as people used to because of cars, planes, bikes, and other modes of transportation. In the Bible, walking is a common theme. In the very beginning, Adam and Eve walked in the garden with God. There was intimacy in those walks: the Creator of the universe and the first humans together. In the Old Testament, those in close relationship with God "walked with God."

Jesus walked all over Israel with his disciples, teaching about the kingdom. Some of their discussions happened while walking along and are recorded in the gospels. Jesus walked up the hill at Calvary, bearing the cross so that you could walk with him as Adam and Eve did in the garden.

Walking is a form of abiding by stepping together. Jesus is inviting you to walk with him. Won't you step out in faith today?

GIFT OF FAITH

"If you believe, you will receive whatver you ask for in prayer."

MATTHEW 21:22 NIV

Isn't it easier when A equals B? Some believers try to take Scriptures, like this one, in that way. If you ask God, and believe hard enough, he will give you what you want. A equals B. Easy math! The danger in this is we might miss what Jesus is really teaching here by not accounting the Bible's teachings as a whole. This view of prayer compromises the sovereignty of God and ignores other parts of Scripture.

Then it gets confusing. Did Jesus not just give us a clear imperative to have faith? Doesn't Jesus want us to pray in faith? Of course he does! But he is not asking you to force yourself into belief. He's asking you to submit your needs and lay them before God. Faith comes from the Spirit as a gift. The very act of prayer gives you the gift of faith.

It's in the drawing near, the asking, the submitting, that faith works in you. It becomes less about getting a specific thing as God makes known to you his will and his way.

ALL YOUR HEART

One of them, an expert in the law, tested him with this question: "Teacher, which is the greatest commandment in the Law?" Jesus replied: "'Love the Lord your God with all your heart and with all your soul and with all your mind.' This is the first and greatest commandment."

MATTHEW 22:34-38 NIV

The Pharisees were always trying to trip up Jesus. They wanted nothing more than to find fault with him—a reason to put him on trial or do away with him. So when they asked him which of all the commandments was the greatest, they were hoping that he would somehow fail to come up with the correct answer.

As usual, Jesus got it right. And, oh, how right it was! When we love the Lord our God with all our hearts, everything else falls into place.

Put God first in your heart and life. Then, when you are tested with myriads of questions, you can trust God to give you the right answer at just the right time.

FEBRUARY

I can do all things through Christ
who strengthens me.

Philippians 4:13 NKJV

PROMISES

"Please, my lord," she said, "as surely as you live, my lord, I am the woman who stood here beside you praying to the Lord. I prayed for this boy, and since the Lord gave me what I asked him for, I now give the boy to the Lord."

1 Samuel 1:26-28 csb

We often pray without expecting much of a response, so it is good to acknowledge those times when we see that God has answered our prayers.

These stories in Scripture help to build our faith and so do the stories of our answered prayers. They are there to be shared. Be encouraged today to continue to present your requests to God, knowing that he is listening.

God answer prayers, although sometimes not the way you want. Continue to remember and share stories where you have witnessed God's answers and let those stories encourage others in their faith.

RIGHTEOUS ANSWERS

By awesome deeds you answer us with righteousness,
O God of our salvation,
the hope of all the ends of the earth
and of the farthest seas.

Psalm 65:5 ESV

What have you been asking of God lately? It could be healing from illness, prayer for someone close to you who is hurting, or maybe you just need a little help in your relationships. It is often said that God hears our prayers; yet you might feel like he has never answered yours.

God can seem very far away and unconcerned with your requests and needs. These feelings, however, are not the truth. The truth is that God is always very near to you. He knows your heart, he knows what you need, and he will answer.

Trust God as you read this Scripture again and know that he will answer your prayers with amazing wonders and inspiring displays of power. Let this increase your faith today.

RIPE

"My food," said Jesus, "is to do the will of him who sent me and to finish his work. Don't you have a saying, 'It's still four months until harvest'? I tell you, open your eyes and look at the fields! They are ripe for harvest."

JOHN 4:34-35 NIV

Food is a necessary part of our existence. Sometimes it feels like we eat to live and live to eat. Jesus explains that doing the will of the Father is necessary and fulfilling. He says that unlike the crops that we wait for, we do not need to wait for souls that need saving, they are already ready.

Jesus wants us to know that there are many still waiting to hear and receive the gospel. Learn to see sharing your salvation as a necessary part of your calling as well.

Thank Jesus for involving you in his plan for humanity by sharing your faith. Ask him for boldness to help reap what has been sown.

SMALL AND SIGNIFICANT

"Truly I tell you, anyone who will not receive the kingdom of God like a little child will never enter it." And he took the children in his arms, placed his hands on them and blessed them.

MARK 10:15-16 NIV

Children may or may not be a part of your family life but you need to remember that they are the future of this world. Children need to be cared for, taught, and shown love so they can one day be the kind of adults that will respect this world and respect others.

We can pass on our faith to the children around us by being adults who show the love of Christ to them. Love and cherish the children who have been put in your life by showing them your faith and teaching them about Jesus.

Pray for the children of the world to find provision, healing, love, value, and purpose. Ask God to bring them to early faith in Jesus.

SOMETHING IS DIFFERENT

If your faith remains strong, even while surrounded by life's difficulties, you will continue to experience the untold blessings of God! True happiness comes as you pass the test with faith, and receive the victorious crown of life promised to every lover of God!

JAMES 1:12 TPT

No one wants to be tested. No one says while life is running along smoothly, "I hope something bad happens soon!" When life feels like one big blessing, we're content with those blessings we have.

Looking back, though, on tests we've gone through and passed, we can see how life is richer—how we are wiser. We can feel, having lived through it, how God drew closer, and that he remains.

Having lived through trials, thank God for them. Thank him for wisdom and a greater measure of faith. Thank him for holding you more tangibly, for proving your trust, and for crowning your life with the blessings reserved for those who call him Lord.

EVERYTHING WITH LOVE

Do everything with love.

1 Corinthians 16:14 NLT

In summary of all Paul had written to the Corinthian believers, he recapped his letter in an almost bullet point fashion. We must stay on our guard and keep vigilant because we have a real enemy who desires for us to fail. The devil will try to tempt us and distract us from the call God has placed on our lives. The way we can distinguish lies is by standing firm in our faith and knowing what God says.

Our courage and strength come from God. He is mighty and will always save us, so we do not need to be afraid. The more intimately we know God, the braver and stronger we will be. Everything can be done in love because God is love, and those who follow God will walk in the way of love.

Why is love more important than any other commandment or any other spiritual gift? Ask God to keep your eyes open and your heart inclined to his voice.

STILL GOOD

I said to Yahweh,
"You are my Maker and my Master.
Any good thing you find in me has come from you."

PSALM 16:2 TPT

Jesus isn't just responsible for the good things in our lives; he's also the author of the good things in us. Your tenderness, humor, and talent? That's Jesus in you. Your faith, perseverance, and loyalty? All the Lord.

You are wonderful. He made you so because he wants you to show the world how wonderful he is. Just by being you, you can lead others closer to him.

List the ways you are special. Ask God to magnify the things that make you attractive to others, so you can reflect his goodness to them.

STRONG AND HEALTHY

I could have no greater joy than to hear that my children are following the truth.

3 JOHN 1:4 NLT

We are all encouraged when we know that the hard work we have put into helping kids learn has been put to good use. Think of the teachers that have seen their children go on to become scientists, world leaders, or missionaries.

What joy to know that we can pass down our knowledge and truth to others, so they can do something good with it.

Ask Jesus to bring people into your life whom you can teach about his Word. Ask him to bring you opportunities, even this week, to do something meaningful that will last for many years to come.

THE LITTLE

Better is the little of the righteous
than the abundance of many wicked.

Psalm 37:16 NASB

The abundance of the wicked may be tantalizing to those of us who have very little, but the little that the righteous have is of far greater value. To gain wealth through evil means is worthless because the days of the wicked are numbered.

Whether the Lord has blessed us with great wealth or taught us to endure with very little, we are to offer what we have to God and find contentment in him alone. This life and its treasures will pass away, so the Lord seeks to increase our faith. All the pleasures of this life pale in comparison to a life lived serving the Lord, for true joy is found in him alone.

How can you choose to be happy with the little you have? Praise God for the eternal inheritance you have in him.

VOICES

"If there arises among you a prophet or a dreamer of dreams, and he gives you a sign or a wonder, and the sign or the wonder comes to pass, of which he spoke to you, saying, 'Let us go after other gods'—which you have not known—'and let us serve them,' you shall not listen to the words of that prophet or that dreamer of dreams, for the LORD your God is testing you to know whether you love the LORD your God with all your heart and with all your soul."

DEUTERONOMY 13:1-3 NKJV

In this present time, it is not necessarily our temptation to go after other gods in the sense of finding someone else to worship. Yet we are still faced with gods of this world, and plenty of temptation to draw near to them.

We love our phones, social media, clothes, house décor, sports—the list is endless. You will be out in the world today with many things calling for your attention, time and money. Try to avoid those words that say, "Let's go after that," and instead direct your heart, mind, and soul toward the one true God.

Ask God to help you go into your day with a clear and focused mind that is centered on what is most important.

WHERE YOU LIVE

LORD, I love the house where you live,
he place where your glory dwells.

PSALM 26:8 NIV

You know that house, the one where every time you're in it you just feel good? It may be picture-perfect, without a pillow out of place or a stray crumb in sight, or it may be the messiest, most mismatched home you know. Decorations and dust bunnies have nothing to do with it: a house feels good when love lives there. When love lives there, so does the Lord.

A home where the Lord's presence is welcome is a home where we feel not just welcome but wanted. There needn't be devotionals on every table or Bible verses stenciled on the walls; his presence dwells in the presence of love—of those who love him.

Ask God to make your home that house. The moment someone walks in your door, ask him to whisper a welcome to their hearts.

WILLING TO TURN

Let the wicked change their ways
and banish the very thought of doing wrong.
Let them turn to the LORD that he may have mercy on them.
Yes, turn to our God, for he will forgive generously.

ISAIAH 55:7 NLT

God loves even the wicked. We were wicked before he washed us clean and changed our hearts. There is no better time to call out to Jesus, confess sins, and rededicate ourselves to him than right now. He would rather we come to him broken and contrite than wait until we feel like we're in a better place. He wants to help us overcome our obstacles.

The Lord is abundantly merciful and generous. He does not hold our pasts against us, and he expects us to let them go as well. If we are willing to turn to him, he is able to turn us from our wicked ways.

Think about what turning to God entails for you.

A TENT MAKER

I have not coveted anyone's silver or gold or clothing. You yourselves know that I worked with my own hands to support myself and those who are with me.

ACTS 20:33-34 CSB

Paul had a lot of support from believers, but he also had to continue to work for himself. Sometimes we think that all Paul did was go from mission to mission; yet at times he had to stay and earn his own money in his profession—as a tent maker.

Whatever you are busy doing today, remember that God not only wants you to be a great missionary for him, but that he values the work that you already do because it is part of his plan for you.

In what ways are you able to support yourself and those in the faith? Be encouraged that God is pleased with your work.

ASK FOR HELP

We can confidently say, "The Lord is my helper; I will not fear; what can man do to me?"

HEBREWS 13:6 ESV

Discouragement and worry come upon all of us from time to time. It may seem that nothing is going well. Someone has defied your authority. Perhaps a supervisor has questioned one of your decisions. Maybe you are battling an ongoing health problem. What we do in this time of despair is an indicator of our simple faith. We turn to God, calling upon his name and asking for his help.

The Bible tells us that God will help us in our time of need. He delights in sending you help. He will lift your burden of worry and care. He will show you a situation differently or provide you with a way around a problem.

Keeping this promise of God in your heart can supply you with confidence to see the day through.

ABIDE IN HIM

His anointing teaches you about everything, and is true, and is no lie—just as it has taught you, abide in him.

1 John 2:27 ESV

As believers, we know that Jesus is the source of all life. We read his Word and learn from it. We soak in knowledge from the truth of what he tells us, and we trust. One thing he asks—that we abide in him. As we grow in spiritual maturity this becomes an easier concept to hold onto.

The principle of abiding and remaining can be a great learning opportunity for someone who is newer in the faith or going through a tough situation. It isn't always easy to keep your eyes on the author of peace or to want to remain with him when you feel lost, confused, or broken.

Encourage other brothers and sisters in Christ in the faith and promise of Jesus.

FEBRUARY 16

ROCK OF SAFETY

Be my rock of safety
Where I can always hide.
Give theo rder to save me,
For you are my rock and fortress.

PSALM 71:3 NLT

There is so much change in our lives on a regular basis. It is difficult to know what we can cling to in a world that is always shifting. When it comes down to it, what are the unshakeable tenets of our faith? God, in his love, makes it clear that he is unchanging. Our understanding of his goodness may fluctuate, sometimes multiple times a day, but his character remains constant.

Where does your confidence lie? Are you relying on your own intelligence, strength, and determination to succeed in life? When all else fails, what is left for you to hold onto?

If you don't have an answer for these questions, let your heart open to the Spirit of wisdom who conveys the mysteries of God to those who ask.

RETURN

"Seek the LORD while he may be found;
call upon him while he is near."

ISAIAH 55:6 ESV

God is a gracious Father. He patiently waits for his children to return to him when they insist on going their own way. When we are lost to our own whims and desires, we will ultimately find that nothing is enough to satisfy the longing of relationship that we have for God. In him we have the goodness that we are looking for.

Have you been trying to find pleasure and fulfillment your own way? There is no time limit to God's mercy. Today is the perfect opportunity to return to your good Father. He welcomes you with open arms whenever you approach.

Do not fear God's judgment; he is full of love and forgiveness, and he will restore everything back to you. It is not too good to be true—it is his promise.

DON'T BE ASHAMED

I am suffering now because I tell the Good News, but I am not ashamed, because I know Jesus, the One in whom I have believed. And I am sure he is able to protect what he has trusted me with until that day.

2 Timothy 1:12 NCV

Have you ever tried to wade upstream through a river, or swim against a strong current? It is hard! Sometimes this is how we feel as Christians in a world full of unbelievers. Our modern culture is full of political correctness and accepting all beliefs, but when it comes to Christianity, it feels like anything we say is offensive!

Paul was put in prison a number of times for offending the people of his time. He seemed to suffer gladly because he was convinced that Jesus was the Savior and that his mission was to share this good news with the world. Paul was convinced of the truth, and because of this, he was not ashamed.

Ask God for confidence to share your faith with others unashamedly. Trust him to protect you as the world becomes more hostile toward him.

FAITH WITH PATIENCE

Be like those who through faith and patience will receive what God has promised.

HEBREWS 6:12 NCV

Patience in practice is never quitting. It does not mean perfectly believing and hoping in every moment. It does not mean never doubting. It is facing the challenge of the present moments that threaten hope and pressing through even if just by sheer determination. Sometimes it looks like being discouraged one night and deciding to keep going the next morning.

God is faithful to fulfill his promises. That will always remain true. His timing, though, is often different than our expectations would dictate. In the face of waiting, do not give up hope.

You will receive what you have been promised. Keep believing even if it means wading through doubt on your way to the promise.

FIRM FAITH

God demonstrates his own love for us in this:
While we were still sinners, Christ died for us.

Romans 5:8 NIV

There is a lot of joy in reminding yourself that you are free from the guilt and punishment of wrongdoing. This is the very reason that Jesus was sent into the world. At the heart of the Christian faith lies our belief in Jesus Christ and his power to save us from sin and death. Eternity is our destiny.

There are things that constantly challenge our faith and we can sometimes lose the power of what we believe when we don't center our thoughts on Jesus. Just as you may ask others to commit important things to memory, you probably have this verse memorized. Take some time today to dwell on what it really means for you.

Thank God for sending his Son into the world so you can receive eternal life. Your belief in Jesus means that you are not condemned.

PALM TREES

The righteous flourish like the palm tree
and grow like a cedar in Lebanon.

Psalm 92:12 ESV

If you live in a cooler climate, you've probably experienced the gorgeous season that is fall. Each year, the leaves slowly turn to shades of golden yellow, orange, and red. It's a thing of beauty, but eventually, the leaves wither and die, then fall to the ground.

All too often, the same can happen in our relationship with the Lord. We get that initial fire for him; we burn brightly with it but lose our way and fall away. If we keep our trust in him, he tells us that our spiritual leaves will never wither. He wants our lives to be like trees that continually bear fruit.

Ask God to help you stand up to the heat and wind and continue to burn brightly for him.

HEROES

"Let your light shine before others, so that they may see your good works and give glory to your Father who is in heaven."

MATTHEW 5:16 ESV

Who are your heroes? Who inspires you? For many young people, heroes are celebrities or sports figures who have a superstar image. When you live a godly life, those around you notice.

You might not know it, but many people look to you as an example. Let your life be an inspiration to them. They need better role models than what media supplies. Show them the love of God through your actions and deeds.

You can see in God's Word how to act and what to do to best shine the light of Jesus to the world. Ask him to give you the enabling power to be a testimony of his glory.

TEXTBOOK OF LIFE

All Scripture is breathed out by God and profitable for teaching, for reproof, for correction, and for training in righteousness, that the man of God may be complete, equipped for every good work.

2 Timothy 3:16-17 ESV

If you had been a teacher during the 18th or 19th centuries, your reading textbook would have been the New England Primer. The ABCs were taught by stories from the Bible, which not only taught the children to read, but gave morals for living as well. Sadly, as secularism infiltrated society, laws were written to remove religious education from our schools. Test scores dropped, morals declined, and crime began to rise.

There is no substitute for the Word of God. It is useful to teach us what is true and to make us realize what is wrong in our lives. It corrects us and teaches us to do what is right. God uses it to prepare and equip his people to do every good work.

What better textbook could there be than one written by God? Be trained by it so you can train others.

WISHFUL THINKING

For in hope we have been saved, but hope that is seen is not hope; for who hopes for what he already sees?

ROMANS 8:24 NASB

We sometimes think of hope as little more than wishing for a favorable option. Granted, if we are unsure of our chances, it seems this might be our only type of hope. The hope of Jesus is sure. The reason we hope is that we cannot see the result of our faith with physical eyes yet. The reason we are sure about this, not just wishing in advance, is that Jesus is trustworthy.

Knowing Jesus helps us to have hope as we abide in him, awaiting the manifestation of his glory. We are so eager to see the King! This hope carries us through life's storms.

Thank God for taking care of things unseen, so you can trust him and enjoy the anticipation of his promises.

OUR PRESENT HOPE

Through Christ you have come to trust in God. And you have placed your faith and hope in God because he raised Christ from the dead and gave him great glory.

1 Peter 1:21 NLT

Our present hope, as sons and daughters of the King, is that God raised Christ Jesus from the dead and has seated him at the right hand of the Father. From this place, Jesus makes intercession for us. He has also raised us up to sit with him in heavenly places! Assured of this hope, we can daily sit with Jesus and agree with him in prayer.

We can be confident that Jesus will perfect all that concerns us as we pray in unity with him for his purposes to be established. Jesus can and will do above and beyond what we ask or imagine, according to the power that works in us. As we let the Holy Spirit take the lead and come into agreement with Jesus for what he desires to see, we will experience breakthrough in areas that seemed impossible.

Place your faith and hope in God, because if God is for you, no one can be against you!

SAVED BY FAITH

"Whoever believes in the Son has eternal life, but whoever rejects the Son will not see life, for God's wrath remains on them."

JOHN 3:36 NIV

When we believe in Jesus, it is more than just choosing in our minds to agree with what we've been told about him. We live aligned with his kingdom truth. We offer him our loyalty and commitment. We trust and rely on his goodness in our lives even as we give ourselves to being united with his character.

When you consider your lifestyle, where do your loyalties lie? When you look at the fruit of your life, is it reflective of what you say you believe? Without judgment, look objectively at what your life reveals as the things you are convinced of.

If there is discrepancy between what you say you believe and how you live, take this opportunity to ask why. Invite the Lord into this part of your processing and allow him to show you the truth of his love over you.

SET ON THE SPIRIT

To set the mind on the flesh is death, but to set the mind on the Spirit is life and peace.

ROMANS 8:6 ESV

When the worries of life overtake our minds, finding peace within it seems impossible. Despair is not far behind the anxieties that send us spiraling. When we focus on the lack of our circumstances, we will feel as if there is no way out, and the desperation to try and do everything we can to fix it will further deplete our emotional resources.

There is another way! When we consider the Holy Spirit and the fruit that he so freely gives, we align ourselves with hope and faith. Let us not be drawn into the spiral of unmet needs; rather, let us look to the unchanging character of our good God who never fails.

God's faithfulness is steady and sure, and you will see his goodness in the land of the living. You will see him come through for you again and again. Believe it!

STEADFAST HOPE

The LORD values those who fear him,
those who put their hope in his faithful love.

PSALM 147:11 CSB

The love of God is steadier than the largest mountain on earth. He will not be swayed away from compassion or mercy—it is who he is. In the same way, we find hope in this unending, unmoving, fiery love. When all seems lost, let us lift our eyes to our lover God who never changes his mind about us.

Hope does not always come easily; it is like warfare to anticipate God's goodness in the face of trials and circumstances that test our belief systems. When it comes down to it, our confidence is not based on our own works or worth; it is based on the God who never changes. Take hope in him today.

God is where all your hopes find their fulfillment. He is the hand that steadies you throughout life. Stay close to him. He will meet you in the middle of your mess and fill your heart with peace.

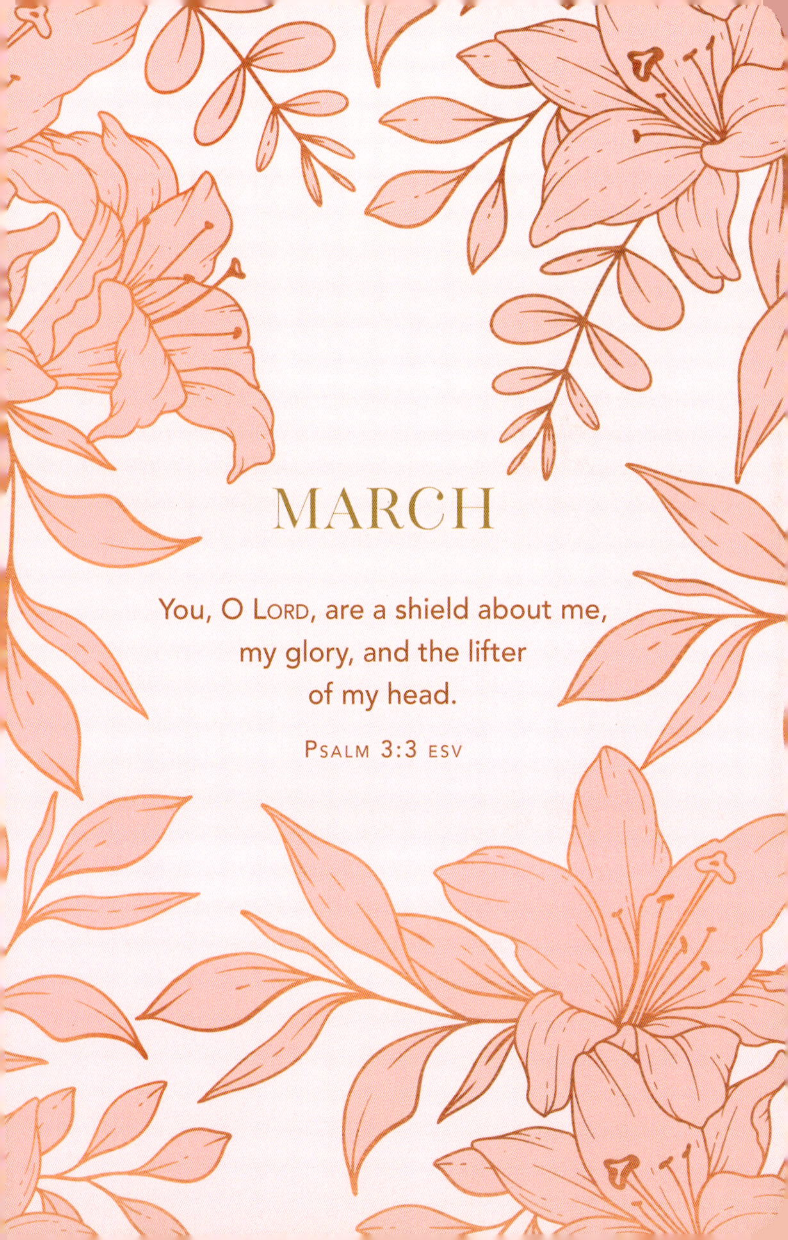

MARCH

You, O Lord, are a shield about me,
my glory, and the lifter
of my head.

Psalm 3:3 esv

BOASTING IN WEAKNESS

If boasting is necessary, I will boast about my weaknesses.

2 Corinthians 11:30 CSB

You are amazing! How did you feel when you read that? Did you feel affirmed, or a bit uncomfortable? Pleased, or patronized? When someone gives you a sincere compliment, are you able to receive it with the same level of sincerity? This is tricky for many of us, as we tread that fine line we've walked since children, the one between graciousness and fear of appearing vain.

One of the many wonderful things about life in Christ is that we can cast this worry aside. Once we grasp that every good thing about us is a gift from him, we are free to appreciate being appreciated. Not only that, we also get to call attention to the awesome work he does through our weak places.

Consider responding to a compliment like this: "Thank you! Let me tell you, that was all God. My human side wanted to run for the hills. I can't believe the courage he gave me to hang in there." Doesn't that feel good?

CHOSEN ONES

You are a chosen race, a royal priesthood, a holy nation, a people for his possession, so that you may proclaim the praises of the one who called you out of darkness into his marvelous light.

1 Peter 2:9 CSB

On occasion, we need a little nudge for all the pieces of our disposition to fall into alignment with God's. Today's nudge is a grand reminder of our identity as a Christian body. We are each holy priests serving the Living God! He is risen, and we are singly and corporately his. Because of this, we each walk in his light, and we shepherd others into the light as well.

Sometimes, it is difficult to get rid of the grumpy feelings of the day. It seems okay to have a lower opinion of ourselves and our circumstances (and maybe other people). But the truth is that God's opinion is our opinion, and we are to shout that in everything we do.

Priests carry a message to the people. What message are you carrying today?

HE REMAINS FAITHFUL

If we are not faithful, he will still be faithful, because he must be true to who he is.

2 TIMOTHY 2:13 NCV

You cry at happy movies, you laugh when you are uncomfortable, and you sneeze when you are nervous. We are who we are.

You can no more change these things about yourself than you can change the number of freckles on your arm. Nor can God change his faithfulness toward you, his love for you, and his unlimited capacity for grace. He is who he is. And oh, aren't you glad?

Only God can be who he is, and that is perfect. Ask God to help you be known for your faithfulness and recognized by your love. Thank him for his faithfulness to you.

HEART OF INTEGRITY

David shepherded them with integrity of heart;
with skillful hands he led them.

PSALM 78:72 NIV

We don't all need to be like David; we aren't all meant to have the same qualities and gifts. God created us to complement one another and to work together for a greater purpose.

We, like David, will all experience brokenness and sin. Yet God can still do great things with our lives when we pursue him. What have you been pursuing today? Perhaps you have been chasing the things of this world, and God is calling you back. Be brave enough to follow him with your heart and your skills.

What has God put in your heart to lead with integrity? What skills has he placed in your hands?

IMAGO DEI

God said, "Let us make man in our image, after our likeness. And let them have dominion over the fish of the sea and over the birds of the heavens and over the livestock and over all the earth and over every creeping thing that creeps on the earth."

GENESIS 1:26 ESV

God created you in his image. Have you ever pondered what this really means? God intended for you and the rest of humanity to demonstrate what he is like to the rest of the world; to display the goodness of the Creator and to represent his name. That's a big task.

Remember that it isn't what you strive to do, it's who you are, so be encouraged today that you are representing your Creator just by being you.

God created you and he loves you. Despite your imperfections, you can still reflect him in your life as you love others.

IN A NAME

Let all who take refuge in you rejoice;
let them ever sing for joy;
and spread your protection over them,
that those who love your name may exult in you.

Psalm 5:11 ESV

Many people do not place a lot of significance on naming. They use names that sound good with last names, re-use family names, mimic characters in a story. Names don't reflect character in our culture. That's why it is easy to think of God as just *God*. One name. But he has many names in the Bible—names that reflect his awesome character. When you dive into the names of God, it's like looking into a multi-faceted diamond, with each new angle reflecting even more light. We can become personally acquainted with his character.

As you fight your battle today, no matter what you are going through, find refuge in the names of God. Call them out loud as a praise offering, acknowledging who you are loved by. And take joy in the fact that as you step out today, you have safety in God.

Look up some names of God today. How can you acknowledge more of who he is through these names?

JESUS REP

Whatever you do, whether in word or deed, do it all in the name of the Lord Jesus, giving thanks to God the Father through him.

Colossians 3:17 NIV

When you work for a company or organization, you are expected to represent that particular brand or identity. Organizations who have a good reputation typically have a culture that their people are committed to being a part of. When you think of that company or brand, you can identify a certain value.

When you become a follower of Jesus, you also become his representative. Your personal relationship with Christ will inspire you to express something of his love, goodness, and grace to the world around you. You don't always need to shout that you are doing things in his name, you just need to simply be aware that your words and actions are influenced by his grace.

Be encouraged today that you will represent him wherever you go.

NO OFFENSIVE WAY

See if there is any offensive way in me
and lead me in the way everlasting.

PSALM 139:24 NIV

Have you taken any personality tests, or tried to figure out what type of person you are? We all know people who are the type to speak their minds even if the words come out offensively. Perhaps you are one of those people! Even if you aren't intentionally trying to cause offense, unfiltered thoughts that land as words can end up being hurtful. If this is one of your vices, take an extra second to think before you speak. It can help to switch that filter on that tells you when you are about to say something rude or unkind.

In the same way, if you are prone to being offended, take a look at the heart of the person who said the wrong thing. Were they really trying to hurt you? Offense is hard, whether you are on the giving or receiving end of it, so allow God's grace to enter those situations.

Ask God to help you in your offense whether you are giving or receiving it. You can be loving and filled with grace for others. He will show you how.

REASSURANCE

The LORD turned to him and said, "Go in the strength you have and save Israel out of Midian's hand. Am I not sending you?" "Pardon me, my lord," Gideon replied, "but how can I save Israel? My clan is the weakest in Manasseh, and I am the least in my family." The LORD answered, "I will be with you, and you will strike down all the Midianites, leaving none alive."

JUDGES 6:14-16 NIV

We compare ourselves to others when assessing our ability to do something. Gideon felt like he was the least according to family hierarchy and his birth order.

God has created each of us as a unique person and he doesn't look at outward factors. Instead God looks at the heart and will use anyone who is willing to trust that God can work through them. It is not about you, but about your willingness to let God work through you.

In what ways do you compare yourself to others? You can trust God to work through you.

SOMETHING DIFFERENT

"I am not asking you to take them out of the world but to keep them safe from the Evil One. They don't belong to the world, just as I don't belong to the world."

JOHN 17:15-16 NCV

We know the out of this world pasta sauce was made right there in our friend's kitchen, and that the singer's otherworldly voice came straight from her lungs. When something is too wonderful to describe, we search for the words to accurately convey its specialness.

As one who belongs to Jesus, you still go to your job, sleep in your bed, and do your best to love well and make a difference, but there is something different about you. You are wonderful in his eyes. A citizen of heaven, you are no longer of this world.

You belong to Jesus. Although you don't belong here, you still live here and this means you need the Father's protection—and he is happy to give it to you.

THE WORLD WILL KNOW

As God's chosen people, holy and dearly loved, clothe yourselves with compassion, kindness, humility, gentleness and patience.

COLOSSIANS 3:12 NIV

Are you wearing compassion today? Did you put on kindness and slip into humility? Don't forget to button up gentleness and patience. Nothing you wear will flatter you the way an outfit of these godly attributes does. Complete the look with head-to-toe love, and you'll be positively glowing.

It's a cute image, and a fun little metaphor, but what if we made it more than that? What if, as we dressed, did our hair, and spritzed on our signature scent, we consciously clothed ourselves in the characteristics that identify us as Christians? How lovely would we be?

Ask God to drape you in compassion and cover you with kindness. Adorn yourself in gentleness and patience and be wrapped in humility. On top of everything, have him decorate you with love.

WIRED FOR CONNECTION

The LORD God said, "It is not good for the man to be alone. I will make a helper suitable for him."

GENESIS 2:18 NIV

We all have our days when we think the world would be simpler if we were all the same: I just don't understand men, we think. They don't always understand women, either, and undoubtedly have the exact same thoughts.

But let's not question God's infallible wisdom for long. Very intentionally, he created two genders—and not just for reproduction. We are different so that we can help, surprise, and complement one another. On the days you momentarily forget this, recall all the lovely ways you know it to be true.

Think of a few of your favorite people and celebrate the ways you are different.

GOD'S WORKMANSHIP

We are God's handiwork, created in Christ Jesus to do good works, which God prepared in advance for us to do.

Ephesians 2:10 NIV

We were fashioned in the image of the Creator. It is in our design to reflect the beauty of God. There is no goodness displayed in our lives that is disconnected from him. When we see the resemblance of love, grace, patience, kindness, and mercy in our lives, we know that we are revealing our Maker.

We are not duplicates or cheap copies of some better model. God has created us each uniquely and wonderfully. We are not meant to be cookie-cutter. That was never the plan. But we were always meant for family. We belong to him. What we do, we do out of a reflection of our good Father.

Align your life with the fullness of his heart which is overflowing with compassion toward you.

THE RIGHT ARMOR

Put on the full armor of God, so that you can take your stand against the devil's schemes.

Ephesians 6:11 NIV

She is so independent; he is so creative; she is such an organized person; I just love what a powerful speaker he is! Compliments stick with us and they can help build the identity of who we think we are. Sometimes our greatest compliments reflect the armor that we have put on to mask our deepest fears. Mrs. Independent is really afraid of being abandoned. Mr. Creativity feels the pressure to always produce. Mrs. Organized needs to hold all the control. Mr. Speaker doesn't know how to speak genuinely with those closest to him.

The armor of God is all about attributes of truth, righteousness, peace, faith, and salvation. These are not just compliments. Who holds this complete set of armor? Jesus. He is our best defense against the schemes of the devil.

Instead of relying on the armor of this world, put on the true armor of God and let him protect you in his mighty power.

YOUR TRUE IDENTITY

If anyone is in Christ, he is a new creation. The old has passed away; behold, the new has come.

2 Corinthians 5:17 esv

What great confidence we have when we know just who we are in Christ! Oh, the benefits and assurance we possess in being grounded in our heavenly Father's advocacy for us. We cannot be separated from his love. When we said yes to Jesus, we awakened our true identity: an identity infinitely grander than we could have imagined.

Now that you live in your new identity, your heavenly Father gazes upon you and sees the righteousness of Christ. God's heart is for you and he encompasses you with his favor. This favor is like a shield—nothing can penetrate it.

Abide with Christ. Enjoy who he is and who he has made you to be.

HUNGER

Poor people will eat until they are full;
those who look to the LORD will praise him.
May your hearts live forever!

PSALM 22:26 NCV

When was the last time you exclaimed, "I'm starving!"? How about, "I'm so full!"? Many of us say both things in a week. Occasionally at the beginning and end of a single meal. Clearly when we examine these terms literally, and in the greater context of a hungry world, we are not starving if we have the means to become full only minutes later. Chances are we can't even begin to understand what that kind of hunger feels like.

So, what are we really saying? We are recognizing, by the empty, gnawing feeling in our bellies, an unmet need. As you take some time out of your busy day, make sure to fill your heart with Jesus so you won't be empty.

You have been given fullness of life. God can and will meet all of your needs. Ask him to fill you with his presence today.

HYPOCRISY

Do everything without complaining and arguing, so that no one can criticize you. Live clean, innocent lives as children of God, shining like bright lights in a world full of crooked and perverse people.

PHILIPPIANS 2: 14-15 NLT

A common complaint against Christians is hypocrisy. People don't see the desired level of perfection, so they label them hypocrites. This causes Christians to either stop trying or hide their faith. The world is a dark place, and it could use some bright light. A pitch-black room is illuminated when even the smallest match is lit. Don't be discouraged in your witness; let your light shine bright. If people claim hypocrisy over you, point them to the beauty of the cross.

When you sin, demonstrating repentance, forgiveness, and grace to a world that isn't fluent in that language speaks a powerful message of light. God is not calling you to live a perfect life. He is asking you to live boldly as a model of forgiveness in a world that is dark.

At work, at school, with your family and your friends, let those whose eyes are so adjusted to the dark see the beauty of God's light in you.

ILLUSION OF CONTROL

Submit therefore to God. But resist the devil and he will flee from you.

JAMES 4:7 NASB

Submit to God and resist the devil. How is it that such straightforward advice seems so difficult to follow? Might it be because our culture suggests the opposite? In movies or shows, a character living by this advice is presented as a novelty, or an oddity, and typically succumbs to the pressure to be normal or fit in.

Until we get this right and submit to the one who wants only peace, goodness, and joy for us, we are under the authority of the one who wants to destroy us. Like a frightened cockroach, he will run once we expose him to the light of God's truth, but not before. Until we stand with God and tell the devil no, he's going to hang around.

Fitting in matters much less than standing proudly next to God. Resist the enemy's lure, and send him scurrying far away.

IN HIS EXAMPLE

Laying your life down in tender surrender before the Lord will bring life, prosperity, and honor as your reward.

PROVERBS 22:4 TPT

Perhaps the reason humility is so hard to achieve is that we so desire its promised reward of honor. Perhaps the reason it's so hard to give up control is that we really want the prosperous, abundant life we are told is waiting.

Focused on the prize, we lose our footing on the path. Doesn't this prove our smallness, our utter need for him? We simply cannot do this without the Lord. The glory and riches we crave are only found in him and in his example. Humbling, isn't it? The humbling sets us on our way.

Only in Jesus can you find the perfection, the blessings, and the glory you strive for. One step at a time, follow his example straight to your reward.

IN OUR SIGHT

Look straight ahead,
and fix your eyes on what lies before you.

Proverbs 4:25 NLT

Have you ever seen a horse wearing blinders? One of the main reasons for this is so they don't get spooked by something off to the side. By focusing strictly on what they see in front of them, they are less vulnerable to distraction and feelings of insecurity from what is going on around them.

God wants us to stay focused, not only so we won't be lured off the path, but so we'll remember that as long as we move forward with him in our sight, we are safe.

How much more peaceful would your life be if you had blinders keeping you from glancing sideways or looking behind? Invite God to narrow your focus to nothing but the path he has set before you.

IT WILL BE DONE

Heal me, LORD, and I will be healed;
Save me and I will be saved,
For You are my praise.

JEREMIAH 17:14 NASB

"If you want to make sure it gets done, ask…." Some people are just known for their reliability. Within an office, a family, a circle of friends, it doesn't take long to figure out who we can count on to make the deadline, host the party, or take out the recycling.

This prayer of Jeremiah's speaks volumes of faith. *Lord, if you do it, it will be done.* With the confidence of God's love, we don't need to wonder. If he takes away the sickness, it's gone. If he mends the wound, it is healed.

With God, your healing is complete and your salvation is forever. Thank him for his unfailing love.

LISTEN TO YOUR HEART

My heart said of you, "Go, worship him."
So I come to worship you, LORD.

PSALM 27:8 NCV

We all have moments where we just need to honor God. Sometimes it's a breathtaking sunset, or a sweet moment with the ones you love the most. It may even be when you're alone in the dark, uninspired by anything seen or felt, but drawn to give him praise.

Awe, gratitude, or longing, to worship him is all the heart wants to do. And when we do worship him? Oh, the sweet, sweet communion we share with our glorious King!

You will never truly be home until you are in heaven, worshipping God for all eternity. May that heart-longing never leave you.

NEVER-ENDING KINGDOM

You are the Lord that reigns over your never-ending kingdom
through all the ages of time and eternity!
You are faithful to fulfill every promise you've made. You
manifest yourself as Kindness in all you do!

Psalm 145:13 TPT

There is nothing we can manufacture here on earth that will stand for eternity. Every earthly kingdom will crumble in time, and only what God has established will remain.

Why should we follow the foolish, short-sighted whims of the world, and waste our hearts and lives building fated kingdoms? Our calling is to a kingdom that will never end, and our investments into that kingdom have eternal worth.

Don't stress and worry about the demands of the daily grind and overlook the importance of relationships and worship. Take a moment to encourage someone or spend a little extra time with God, remembering how much value he assigns to those eternal investments.

NO OTHER GOSPEL

I am astonished that you are so quickly deserting the one who called you to live in the grace of Christ and are turning to a different gospel—which is really no gospel at all. Evidently some people are throwing you into confusion and are trying to pervert the gospel of Christ.

Galatians 1:6-7 NIV

In Paul's time, it was vitally important that people believed and shared the pure truth of the gospel. They did not have the fortune of the written gospel and therefore had to rely on the testimony of the apostles. It was imperative that this gospel was preserved by the church.

These days we have so many different versions of truth and plenty of people who want to change the message of Christ. Don't forget to reference the wonderful Word of God when you need to be reminded of the truth.

Ask God to protect you from the confusion that others may try to throw at you about his good news. Have faith in his Word and diligently remind yourself of Scripture, so the truth of the gospel can remain pure in my heart.

NO OTHER NAME

There is salvation in no one else! God has given no other name under heaven by which we must be saved.

Acts 4:12 NLT

The one thing that the people in Jesus' day needed was salvation, yet they crucified the only person who could offer it. They didn't believe that Jesus was the Messiah.

We live in a society where people typically don't believe that Jesus is the only way to salvation. We have to struggle against a concept that all truths can be accepted. Remember this Scripture and hold firm to your faith. It is Jesus, and only Jesus, who saves.

Don't be complacent about your faith and take on the world's view that there are many truths. Jesus is the only way. Be secure in this knowledge and share it with others when you get the chance.

OPEN DOOR

Devote yourselves to prayer, being watchful and thankful. And pray for us, too, that God may open a door for our message, so that we may proclaim the mystery of Christ, for which I am in chains. Pray that I may proclaim it clearly, as I should.

COLOSSIANS 4:2-4 NIV

We should always pray that God will open doors for us to share his message. You might not be in a distant land to proclaim the gospel, or in chains for trying to preach the good news, but there are plenty of people who are.

Think of those people who are intent on furthering the kingdom, and devote yourself to praying for them. God is using people in many parts of the world to spread the gospel and reveal his truth.

Pray for wisdom and open doors today. Ask God to show you who would be the most receptive to hearing his Word, and then share it with them!

PEACEFUL TRUTH

The God of peace will soon crush Satan under your feet.
The grace of our Lord Jesus be with you.

ROMANS 16:20 NIV

Have you ever met someone who is afraid that God is out to crush them? Maybe you struggle with this fear yourself. In this verse, there are two interesting descriptive words. Peace and crush. Which is directed at whom? It says, "the God of peace." We are at peace with God by faith in Christ's work on the cross. Who is being crushed? Satan!

This is a fulfillment of the promise made all the way back in Genesis 3:15. We are not to live in fear that God is out to get us. We can be confident of the peace we have found with God in Christ. With this in mind, we want to keep ourselves innocent of evil.

Do not let the one who will be crushed accuse you any longer. You are at peace with God, and he desires to draw near to you.

REMEMBER

Remember the wondrous works that he has done,
his miracles, and the judgments he uttered.

Psalm 105:5 ESV

We are called to pause and remember the works of God. A Hebrew was trained to look back and recount the works God had done in Israel for themselves and for their children. This was foundational in their lifestyle of worship. This word isn't just for them though. We are called to remember the works and miracles that have been recorded. Why should we take time to remember them? Because by nature, we will forget.

When we remember what God has done over time, it removes the anxiety and fear of what he will do in the future. It also reveals his characteristics of love and provision. It tells us that the same God who miraculously split the Red Sea and raised the dead is still moving today.

Remember today what God has done for you. There is no one like him.

THIRSTY SOUL

I long to drink of you, O God,
to drink deeply from the streams of pleasure
flowing from your presence.
My longings overwhelm me for more of you!

Psalm 42:1 TPT

Our physical nature is not separate from our spiritual life. Sometimes when we are in such great need physically it's like our whole being is hungry, thirsty, or in pain. This is how David felt when he was in the wilderness—desperate for real food and water yet feeling like his soul needed the same nourishment.

Waking up this morning, what did you feel like you needed? You probably aren't in the actual wilderness, but perhaps you needed a shower, coffee, or some breakfast. Let your needs today compel you to feel that same need for Christ.

Crave God the same way your body craves what it needs. Acknowledge that you desperately need him today.

TRAIN TO WIN

Don't you realize that in a race everyone runs, but only one person gets the prize? So run to win! All athletes are disciplined in their training. They do it to win a prize that will fade away, but we do it for an eternal prize. So I run with purpose in every step. I am not just shadowboxing.

1 Corinthians 9:24-26 NLT

Apathy is a very real struggle. It can be hard to get motivated for work, cleaning up the house, or getting your assignments done. God doesn't want us to be apathetic in our faith. We can easily become distracted by things in life that don't matter as much as eternity.

Paul is suggesting here that we run to win, not just to endure life but to do the very best that we can. It's not about competition; it is about enthusiasm.

Thank God for the day you've been given. Look for the value of eternity in the little things you do for him. Ask him for energy each day to run this race of faith.

PRAISING TOGETHER

I know that you are most holy; it's indisputable.
You are God-Enthroned, surrounded with songs,
living among the shouts of praise of your princely people.

Psalm 22:3 NLT

Have you had time to reflect on God yet today? You might agree that his holiness is indisputable and yet sometimes it doesn't feel like we revere him like we should.

It can be helpful to put on some music that is glorifying to God. Sometimes the songs and words that other people have written are exactly what you need to help you direct your thoughts and heart toward this amazing God.

What is your favorite worship music, artist, or band? Try listening to something today that will direct your praise to God.

APRIL

It is by grace you have been saved,
through faith—
and this is not from yourselves,
it is the gift of God—
not by works,
so that no one can boast.

Ephesians 2:8-9 NIV

ANCHORED IN TRUTH

The word of the LORD holds true,
and we can trust everything he does.

PSALM 33:4 NLT

Coming home from a day of interacting with other people can leave you wondering what truth really is. People are not always honest about what they think. You might have overheard conversations, or even been involved in conversations, where people are secretly expressing how they feel about a matter, rather than voicing it directly to the person who asked.

This kind of masking of the truth doesn't belong in the Christ's kingdom, and it doesn't reflect the person of Jesus. His Word is true. And because it is true, you can trust him one hundred percent of the time.

Anchor yourself in God's truth so you are not misguided by the untruths of the people around you. Reflect the real truth so you can be trustworthy.

LOSING COURAGE

The ships were tossed as high as the sky
and fell low to the depths.
The storm was so bad that they lost their courage.

Psalm 107:26 NCV

Sometimes it feels like life is tossing you around. Remember that it is not your circumstances that determine your anxiety, it is your faith. Pray for wisdom. But when you do, make sure you are ready to receive it.

Believe the word that the Lord has for you, and do not doubt. If you get stuck on a task or decision today, ask for God's wisdom. He promises to give it to you, and to give liberally.

You can have faith in God's love and care for you in the middle of life's storms. He will keep your heart steady and peaceful through the trouble.

BE BRAVE

In God, whose word I praise—
in God I trust and am not afraid.
What can mere mortals do to me?

Psalm 56:4 NIV

In God We Trust. This is still printed on US currency despite many people not truly having trust, or even a belief in God. As Christians, we claim to trust God.

Is this a motto that is written on the currency of your heart, one that you can hold fast to in times when all else seems to be against you? You might spend some money today. If you do, remind yourself of your trust in God as you hand over your cash.

In the times you don't hear God and you're not sure of what he is leading you toward, choose to trust because he is a God who keeps his word.

BELIEVE IN THE SON

"Whoever believes in him is not condemned, but whoever does not believe stands condemned already because they have not believed in the name of God's one and only Son."

JOHN 3:18 NIV

It really is as simple as believing. We can often approach faith with the idea that we need to be better people. Sometimes we expect others to be better, to do better, to live more of a righteous life. It's important that we live in God's ways, but more importantly is our faith in Jesus. This belief is what saves us, and what saves every other person.

When you love God, you will be better, not through your effort, but through the revelation of love that God shares with you because you believe.

All God requires from your heart is a belief that he is the Son of God and that he came to save you. You are made righteous through this belief.

CELEBRATE

They celebrate your abundant goodness
and joyfully sing of your righteousness.

PSALM 145:7 NIV

God is not a hype or a fad. He is not a popular celebrity who will fade in time from our memories, unable to hold the interest of our children, and unheard of by our children's children. God's name has been proclaimed on the earth throughout every generation, and it always will be.

God's people, old and young, rejoice because of who God is and what he's done. This spans all ages across the globe. We can celebrate God on our own, in our hearts, declaring his righteousness and singing his praises.

God is more than enough reason to celebrate. He has shown his abundant goodness. Be filled with joy because of his righteousness.

CHOOSE HIS WAY

"Take My yoke upon you and learn from Me, for I am gentle and humble in heart, and you will find rest for your souls. For My yoke iscomfortable, and My burden is light."

MATTHEW 11:29-30 NASB

Imagine you're volunteering to work on a farm for a few days, and you get to choose your job. Would you like to break up and move boulders to prepare the field for plowing and planting, or would you prefer to walk behind the plow scattering seeds? Which is more appealing: the back-breaking heavy lifting or the steady purposeful stroll?

Unless we're trying hard to impress someone, or are gluttons for punishment, we're going to choose the seeds, right? This is exactly what it's like to walk with Christ. We can choose his way, and find rest for our souls, or we can go our own way and try to lift those heavy boulders.

The choice to do life God's way is the best choice. When you are tempted to take the harder way, ask him to remind you of his gentle way and invite you, again, to choose it.

CONGREGATION

Praise the LORD!
I will thank the LORD with all my heart
as I meet with his godly people.

PSALM 111:1 NLT

When we turn to God, we are in unity with the rest of the body of Christ. We all have different ways of expressing our faith, yet we all have the same purpose to glorify God.

Have you approached life with stubbornness, unwilling to move or let someone else get their way? God desires unity so he can work through you. Don't let your pride get in the way of unity with others. Let God remove the stones of your heart and be open and responsive to his ways as you move forward.

Don't ignore the gentle whispers of the Holy Spirit. Allow your heart to be guided by him.

CONVINCED

What you heard from me, keep as the pattern of sound teaching, with faith and love in Christ Jesus. Guard the good deposit that was entrusted to you—guard it with the help of the Holy Spirit who lives in us.

2 Timothy 1:13-14 NIV

Do you tend to keep quiet about your faith in Jesus? Are you worried about suffering, or being mocked for your beliefs?

Take time each day to develop your relationship with him; the more you know Jesus, the more confident you will be in what you believe. Imitate Paul's dedication to sharing the gospel, guard its truth, and trust God to protect you.

Spend more time with God so you become as convinced as Paul was that he is the way, the truth, and the life. When you start to share your faith, don't worry about the words you need to speak, God cares more about a genuine heart.

CORNERSTONE

You are coming to Christ, who is the living cornerstone of God's temple. He was rejected by people, but he was chosen by God for great honor.

1 Peter 2:4 NLT

The cornerstone, otherwise known as a foundation stone or setting stone, is the first stone set in the construction of a building's foundation and vitally important since all other stones will be set in reference to this stone. The position of this stone determines the position of the entire structure.

When Christ is referred to as the cornerstone, we know that his life, death, and resurrection is our reference point for how we should live. When we align ourselves with Christ, we are building up that living temple to be used for great honor.

Ask God to show you how you can be used as part of his spiritual temple.

EASIER THAN BREATH

Jesus looked at them and said to them, "With men this is impossible, but with God all things are possible."

MATTHEW 19:26 NKJV

As with so many of Jesus' teachings, context is important. Here, Jesus was talking about the heart. A wealthy young man had just asked him what he needed to do to assure his place in heaven. After Jesus explained he'd need to give up all his wealth, the young man went away. The price was too high.

Concerned no one could be good enough to get into heaven, the disciples asked Jesus if anyone could do enough. "Only God," he told them. Only God can change a heart enough for heaven. And he will, the moment we ask him.

Don't feel defeated knowing you can never be good enough for heaven on your own. Only his heart is pure enough for heaven's glory, so only he can make you worthy. And he will.

FELLOWSHIP

If we claim to have fellowship with him and yet walk in the darkness, we lie and do not live out the truth.

1 John 1:6 NIV

Our lives are consistent with our beliefs. It is not our good works which save us, but someone who has truly been saved will reflect it in the way they live. If nothing has changed in the way we act and we continue to sin, we have deceived ourselves if we believe we walk with God.

This understanding does not permit us to cast judgment on others, since it is the Lord alone who can know the condition of someone's heart. This also does not mean we will be freed from temptation or rid of sin in an instant. God has grace on us while we are being sanctified.

Knowing God and having fellowship with him redeem your heart and mind. You will no longer live for yourself because you have found one who is so much greater.

FOUNTAIN OF LIFE

The fountain of life flows from you to satisfy me.
In your light of holiness we receive the light of revelation.

PSALM 36:9 TPT

To quench your thirst, you need clean, fresh water—and lots of it! This is the way that Jesus can satisfy your soul. His ways are pure and fresh and he offers in abundance. Spend some time getting to know him. This might mean reading Scripture about what he did and said, or conversing with him about your life.

When you understand God's heart for humanity and his heart for you, you will experience joy like nothing else. Let this joy illuminate his ways and give you fresh revelation on your journey of faith.

Press in to knowing God deeper so you can drink in his life and be fully satisfied.

FULLY ARMED

Put on every piece of God's armor so you will be able to resist the enemy in the time of evil. Then after the battle you will still be standing firm.

EPHESIANS 6:13 NLT

Whether you feel victorious about your days or not, God is with you the entire time. Even if you come home feeling emotionally or spiritually battered and bruised, know that you have fought well because you were wearing your spiritual armor.

Battles are part of life, but fending off the darkness that threatens to steal our joy can be wearying. You can find strength in God's Word and in the knowledge of his truth. He will be faithful to restore you.

Resisting temptation and defeating discouragement can leave you tired. Ask God to refresh you so you will continue to stand firm in your faith and in all circumstances.

GOOD NEWS

If you openly declare that Jesus is Lord and believe in your heart that God raised him from the dead, you will be saved. For it is by believing in your heart that you are made right with God, and it is by openly declaring your faith that you are saved.

ROMANS 10:9-10 NLT

If you're wondering how to boil your faith down for someone, to explain it simply and succinctly, this, right here, is the famous good news. There is no complicated set of rules to adopt, no ceremony, no sacrifice required. Believing in Jesus' resurrection wipes your slate clean with God, and saying it out loud assures you a place in heaven.

It is good news, isn't it? The most important decision we'll ever make, the most important sentence we'll ever speak, and it's simple. There is no script, trick, or catch. There is only faith, and the courage to speak it aloud.

Believe and speak of the incomprehensible love God showed by sending his Son to suffer on behalf of all your sins—confessed and unconfessed, past and future.

HE'S THE ONE

"Go and report to John what you hear and see: The blind receive their sight, the lame walk, those with leprosy are cleansed, the deaf hear, the dead are raised, and the poor are told the good news."

MATTHEW 11:4-5 CSB

There were many people in Jesus' time who wanted to know if Jesus was truly the one they had been waiting for. Jesus had been prophesied about and although many wanted to believe he was the one, they still had doubts. Even John the Baptist asked if Jesus really was the one.

It is good to remind ourselves that Jesus really is the one who came to save us all from the curse of sin. He is our redeemer; he is the one who brought healing and salvation to the world.

You might need this solid reminder today. Read this Scripture in faith—Jesus is the one.

PENETRATING WORD

The word of God is alive and active. Sharper than any double-edged sword, it penetrates even to dividing soul and spirit, joints and marrow; it judges the thoughts and attitudes of the heart.

HEBREWS 4:12 NIV

If we were to look at our lives today, would we say we live up to the standard of what the Bible says believers possess and do? Chances are good that we fall short here and there. The phrase, "joints and marrow" refers to the difference between what we are doing and what gives us life.

Where do you go through the motions because society says you must do something different than your heart tells you? Your marrow gives your heart life-giving blood; your God-given desires feed God's will in your life, and he has gifted you toward this end. Move in that direction so your joints will not ache. It is better for man to be dissatisfied with you than for you to miss those good things God has. Get into the Bible and discover them.

Submit to the Lord in choosing the actions that maximize your vitality and your dependence on him.

THE SWORD

Nothing in all creation is hidden from God's sight. Everything is uncovered and laid bare before the eyes of him to whom we must give account.

HEBREWS 4:13 NIV

As we read the stories of the Bible, we search for the truth woven throughout every word in Scripture, and make sure to pay attention. When we increase our knowledge of the stories of Israel, the warnings of the prophets, the sayings of the wise, and the life of Jesus, we are more connected to our faith.

Don't be ignorant in this Christian walk, use the sword (the Word of God) to arm yourself to fight for the faith. Nothing is hidden from God. He sees and knows everything and he rules with perfect justice and mercy.

Ask the Holy Spirit to give you inspiration as you read the Bible. Look for deeper truth and get life from what you read.

LIGHT AND MOMENTARY

Our light and momentary troubles are achieving for us an eternal glory that far outweighs them all.

2 Corinthians 4:17 NIV

It can be hard to be in the middle of turmoil and see your situation as light and momentary. Paul had persecution, imprisonment, church conflict, false teaching, and a myriad of other troubles to deal with; yet, he was able to find his perspective in fixing his eyes on the eternal hope in Christ.

Your situation and particular difficulty is important to Jesus; never undermine your emotional stress. But don't lose heart because Jesus is doing something deeper, better, and eternal. These Scriptures encourage you to look beyond and above your circumstances to find hope. If you stare too hard at where your feet are going, you may miss the joy of looking at the end destination.

Choose today to lift your eyes beyond your own discouragement, struggles, and pain, and be encouraged that it will all be worth it in the end.

LET WISDOM POUR

"To those who listen to my teaching, more understanding will be given. But for those who are not listening, even what little understanding they have will be taken away from them."

MARK 4:25 NLT

Imagine a runner who trains for a marathon, completes it, and then stops running. After a year has gone by, she remembers how much fun she had on race day—how satisfying it felt to cross the finish line feeling strong and accomplished. She shows up to run the marathon the next year but, several miles in, she realizes she won't make it. She's lost her base. To go the distance, you can't just want to run; you need to train.

Following Christ is similar. You need to build—and maintain—your base. If you want to follow Christ, you have to be a Christ-follower. Read your Bible. Pray for understanding. Put what you learn into practice every day.

From the solid base of God's Word, more of the world makes sense. You are strong. You can go the distance.

FAVOR

The Lord God is a sun and shield;
the Lord bestows favor and honor.
No good thing does he withhold
from those who walk uprightly.

Psalm 84:11 ESV

Here we are, right before the official beginning of summer. Summer days are marked by more sunlight. We enjoy its warmth and vitamin D, and we relish in the extra time we can spend outside. Just like the sun, God is always present to nourish us and enlighten our paths.

This metaphor between God and the sun is nowhere else in the Old Testament. Perhaps the prominence of sun worship at the time rendered it a poor metaphor, but what the psalmist is communicating is that not everyone receives the favor of God. If you live in a basement with no windows, and you never come out, you will never receive the favor of the sun. You live in darkness. But if you go outside, there are many benefits, some of which we already listed. God isn't playing favorites, but those who have faith in his Son are walking in the light.

God has many good blessings and honor that he wants to give you. Bask in the warmth of his love today.

HE CALMS MY SOUL

He awoke and rebuked the wind and said to the sea, "Peace! Be still!" And the wind ceased, and there was a great calm.

Mark 4:39 ESV

When we are overcome with worry, let us remember that God is not. Jesus was not worried about the storm when his disciples woke him up in the boat. Clearly, this was no small storm; it was a raging squall. They were worried for their very lives. But Jesus, commanding the winds and waves to be still, was not for a moment concerned. In fact, if we continue in this passage, we see that Jesus was instead perplexed at the lack of his disciples' faith.

What areas of our lives feel so threatened and exposed that we question the very nature of our God? Let us align our hearts with his and trust through faith that we will not be destroyed. What's more, in our helplessness, we are not actually powerless. He who is able to calm the fiercest storm has given us authority to calm the storms around us with his peace, as well.

God is not just powerful to save, he is also the one who stills the chaos. Ask him to speak stillness to the storms that rage in your mind.

NOURISH

"People do not live by bread alone, but by every word that comes from the mouth of God."

MATTHEW 4:4 NLT

We take the time to feed our bodies. Even if we are running late, we hit up the drive-through and grab breakfast. We diet and meal plan, giving a lot of focus to the food that our body consumes. It's not a bad thing to do so, but let's feed our souls with the same remembrance and fervor with which we feed our physical bodies.

We aren't surprised when we get hangry (which is anger as a result of hunger) or weak when we don't eat. Why are we surprised at the direction of our day when we starve our souls? Let us prioritize Scripture and consume the Word of God each day.

Nourish your soul for growth by reading, memorizing, writing, and studying the Scriptures.

BELIEVE IN JESUS

"Will you never believe in me unless you see miraculous signs and wonders?"

JOHN 4:48 NLT

As wonderful as it is to be amazed at Christ's miracles and to witness his wonders, they are not what faith is based on. Anyone who truly desires God and wants to know him personally will read his Word and take it to heart. Those who do will discover that the entire thing, from cover to cover, was written about Jesus Christ and his divinity. The Old Testament is a constant foreshadowing of the Messiah, and the New Testament is a testimony of his life.

If we cannot read and recognize that the only possible, honest conclusion we can draw is that Jesus Christ is God himself, then no number of miraculous signs and wonders will convince us either. We either believe Jesus is who he said he is, or we don't. We are either ready to accept the truth laid out in the Scriptures, or we are not.

Tell Jesus you believe in him whether you see his miraculous signs and wonders or not. You never know what he is doing behind the scenes.

GET WISDOM

The beginning of wisdom is this: Get wisdom.
Though it cost all you have, get understanding.

Proverbs 4:7 NIV

Wisdom comes from God alone; in order to grow in wisdom, we must seek God. Wisdom is different than mere intelligence or knowledge; it is having the mind of Christ. Wisdom supersedes common sense and even intuition. It is of higher value than anything the world boasts of.

If our entire lives were spent in the pursuit of wisdom—truly, the pursuit of God—they would be lives well spent. No amount of riches or fame is worth surrendering our search for wisdom, and understanding its value is the first sign of a wise person.

Although it may take everything you have and cost you greatly in other areas, following God and becoming wise is worth more than everything else.

HOPE IN GOD

Why am I discouraged? Why is my heart so sad?
I will put my hope in God! I will praise him again—
my Savior and my God!

Psalm 42:11 NLT

It is sad to see the way we hurt each other. We are surrounded by sickness and death. The immorality we witness in human trafficking, pornography, and corruption is overwhelming. But God is good and faithful. We have an opportunity each day to put our hope in God, who holds the whole world in his hands.

It is critical that we don't allow the evil in this world, stress, or the monotony of life to weigh on us. We need to put our hope in God and praise him for what he has done and is able to do. There are plenty of reasons to be sad and upset; be encouraged to hope in the goodness of God.

Ask Jesus to quicken your soul with his presence. Give your sadness and frustration to him as you put your faith in his goodness.

HE IS WILLING

It happened when He was in a certain city, that behold, a man who was full of leprosy saw Jesus; and he fell on his face and implored Him, saying, "Lord, if You are willing, You can make me clean."

Luke 5:12 NKJV

What faith and boldness this man with leprosy had. There is little doubt that he had heard of the miracles Jesus could perform, yet there would have been many who doubted his power. This man, however, saw Jesus and immediately believed in God's power and expected to be healed.

You may have seen a lot of unanswered prayer that leaves you with doubts about what God can do, but faith is believing that if God is willing, he can make it happen.

Have the kind of faith today that can expect good and powerful things to happen in your life and in the lives of others.

MATURITY

Solid food is for the mature, who by constant use have trained themselves to distinguish good from evil.

HEBREWS 5:14 NIV

Babies are fed, coddled, and given special baby food. When someone first comes to faith in Christ, they cannot be expected to grasp complex concepts immediately. There is grace for that, for sanctification is a journey. As babies mature into children and eventually adults, however, they are expected to wean off baby food and eat more substantial food.

The same process is true for a Christian. We should not be apathetic or lazy. Through time with God, study of his Word, fellowship with other believers, and the testing of our faith, we mature and should embrace the progression.

God does not expect you to understand everything right away, but he also won't allow you to plateau where you are. He constantly encourages you to take the next bite and grow.

SALT AND LIGHT

"You are the light of the world—like a city on a hilltop that cannot be hidden. No one lights a lamp and then puts it under a basket. Instead, a lamp is placed on a stand, where it gives light to everyone in the house."

MATTHEW 5:14-15 NLT

As you prepare yourself for bed, the last thing you will probably do is turn out the lights. You need the light to see everything you are doing until then. You need the light to show you the way. There would be no point of turning on the light only to cover it up.

This is our journey of salvation. Jesus didn't want you to receive his light and then hide it. He wants you to shine brightly so others will also see the path to faith.

As you reflect on those places where you have hidden your light, thank God for his grace. He understands and he wants to give you the boldness to live out your faith as brightly as you can.

CHARACTER

We also glory in our sufferings, because we know that suffering produces perseverance; perseverance, character; and character, hope. And hope does not put us to shame, because God's love has been poured out into our hearts through the Holy Spirit, who has been given to us.

Romans 5:3-5 NIV

It is hard to square off in the face of suffering; put on a smile and walk directly into that storm. Nobody looks at suffering every time and says, "I would really like more of that!" Suffering is painful. It chips away at our resolve. It can rock our faith. Ironically, it is the very tool that can strengthen our faith as well.

One of the things that sets apart those who thrive is the ability to stay in righteous intimacy with God throughout the duration of the test. This is when the hearts of the believers are steeled. They become patient, grow in character, and embody hope in the face of trial. When suffering takes place, the weight of the burden becomes too great for the believer to bear while juggling other unnecessary baggage. The process of refining sloughs off those weights, and the believer is renewed in a way that no other event could ever trigger.

Ask God to help you see the opportunities in suffering that will bring you closer to him and the destiny he has for you.

JUST BELIEVE

Jesus paid no attention to what they said. He told the synagogue leader, "Don't be afraid; just believe."

MARK 5:36 NCV

Can faith move mountains? Most certainly! The question is, can *your* faith move mountains? Can you trust God to handle momentous things in your life? When the doctor says, "Cancer," when the call comes to tell you of your father's heart attack, when you open the envelope and the note inside says "Terminated," or when the fish tank breaks and spills ten gallons of fishy water all over your cream-colored rug, the right thing to do is turn it over to God. You may wrestle for a long time or you may send up a quick prayer, but give it to him.

Jesus says, "Don't be afraid; just believe." Believe that he will give you the support you need, the wisdom to make the right decisions, and the strength to carry them out. The world has it all backwards. Following God is not an arduous journey along a bomb-strewn path. The answer is simple: believe. Believe that Jesus is the Son of God, that he died to save you from your sins, that he wants to give you life abundantly, and that he has a very special place for you in heaven.

Simply believe. The mountains will move, or God will help you go around them. It's that easy.

MAY

Surely you have granted him
unending blessings
and made him glad
with the joy of your presence.

Psalm 21:6 NIV

VICTORY WON

Every child of God defeats this evil world, and we achieve this victory through our faith.

1 JOHN 5:4 NLT

Life can sometimes feel like the rush to a gate at the airport. You are clambering along with all your bags, moving as quickly as you can. Glancing to the side, you see people working less with just as many bags yet going significantly faster than you! How is that possible? Looking down, you see they are on a moving sidewalk while your feet reside on solid ground.

In life, if you glance to the right or the left it's easy to fall into the comparison trap. It seems like everyone else is getting ahead and you are being left behind. The truth is that, as a believer, you get ahead by faith. Victory has already been won for you! You have a loving Father who has a plan for you.

Keep yourself submitted to God and he will lift your heavy bags and get you where he wants you to go (where he gets the most glory!) right on time.

FAMILY VALUES

If a believer fails to provide for their own relatives when they are in need, they have compromised their convictions of faith and need to be corrected, for they are living worse than the unbelievers.

1 Timothy 5:8 TPT

Giving to charity, volunteering at church, and helping out at a mission are all very important ways of expressing our faith. Why then does this Scripture seem to be so harsh about not helping our own family out? God created the family unit, and even though sin has a way of making them dysfunctional, they are still an important part of who we are. They are also one of the best examples of unconditional love.

The bond you have with your family should be treasured. If you are struggling with forgiveness for a relative, ask Christ to help you. One of the best ways you can mend a relationship is by offering a word of kindness or a hand to help. You might be surprised at how quickly a situation can turn when you prioritize your family.

Pray for a family relationship today. Ask God to restore, strengthen, or renew your love for each other.

WHEN I AM

When I am afraid,
I will put my trust in You.
In God, whose word I praise,
In God I have put my trust;
I shall not be afraid.
What can mere mortals do to me?

PSALM 56:3-4 NASB

We can turn our realities into prayers, acknowledging how we are feeling in the moment while also turning our attention to the Lord. When fear comes knocking on the doors of our hearts, how will we respond? When we are overwhelmed by responsibilities that seem to go on without end, how can we get grounded in the peace of God?

What have you been struggling with lately? Is it frustration, worry, or feeling out of control? Turn them into prayers, just as the psalmist did. "When I am frustrated, I will..." "When I am worried, I will..." "When I am feeling out of control, I will..." Put your trust in the Lord and remind your heart how faithfully good he is.

Take time now to write a script for your day. With intention, you can lead your heart toward the Lord, even as he reaches out to meet you.

BE STRONG

Be strong in the Lord and in his mighty power.

Ephesians 6:10 NLT

Paul did not undercut the importance of the spiritual battles we engage with. He wrote often about how we are in a war against evil and cautioned us to be alert to it. Just prior to describing a detailed metaphor of suiting up in spiritual armor with each of its specific components, he gave the most necessary piece of battleplan advice: "Be strong in the Lord."

God is ready and willing to give us everything we need for any situation. Often, however, he will wait for us to ask, so we are reminded that he is our source of strength and that we should always be turned toward him.

God's strength and power are what win the battles and carry you through each day. When you are attacked or confronted with evil, he will equip you with his strength and spiritual armor.

ALWAYS READY

Pray in the Spirit at all times with all kinds of prayers, asking for everything you need. To do this you must always be ready and never give up. Always pray for all God's people.

EPHESIANS 6:18 NCV

When we live with surrendered hearts to God and an open line of communication, we will always be ready to pray. In every circumstance, every challenging situation, and every season of calm, may we present our pleas to God. Even when our lives are at rest, there will be others walking through the fire of testing. May we pray with compassion and fierce faith on their behalf.

Will you keep your eyes open to the needs of others? Will you lift your prayers to God and turn your attention to his faithfulness and power? When you are weak, the grace of God comes through his Spirit to strengthen you. When you do not know how to pray, the Spirit will intercede on your behalf. When you are at a loss, Jesus never is.

Partner with the Lord in prayer and see how your faith grows.

A HOLY CALLING

Then the king was very glad and gave orders for Daniel to be lifted up out of the den. So Daniel was lifted up out of the den, and no injury whatever was found on him, because he had trusted in his God.

Daniel 6:23 NASB

With every year of life, trust becomes harder to give. Before we've even gone to school, we've learned a hard truth: the world is not entirely safe. The only truly trustworthy thing in this world is not of this world—God. In our minds, we know this. We're called to trust him and deep down we know we can, but there are days when it's hard to live this out.

Rarely has one been more called to trust in God than Daniel. From the moment he was taken from his home to be a slave in Babylon, his belief in God's faithfulness was tested, and never more so than in the lion's den. We know the outcome: he came out completely unscathed. Daniel's trust was rewarded, and his story became a reason for our own.

Pray for the faith of Daniel. Whatever God asks of you, do it with the trust of one who knows he will protect you. Your faith will be rewarded.

DARING FAITH

Joshua spared Rahab the prostitute, with her family and all who belonged to her, because she hid the men Joshua had sent as spies to Jericho—and she lives among the Israelites to this day.

JOSHUA 6:25 NIV

The book of Joshua holds the story of Rahab. Joshua had sent spies to Jericho, Rahab's hometown, to figure out a way to attack. The spies, however, didn't make it out of the city before guards were alerted to their presence. Rahab hid them and lied to the officials searching for them, protecting the spies. In exchange, she asked that she and her family be spared from the impending destruction of the city.

The author points out to us that not only was Rahab a Canaanite, but she was also a prostitute. However, God honored her daring faith, and she is one of just five women to be mentioned in the lineage of Jesus. Rahab heard what the Israelites God had done for them, and she chose to serve him. It was a daring move on her part, turning from her entire culture and life to serve God.

You are often called to go against culture and society to do what you know is right. Be like Rahab: flawed but bold in Christ.

SEEK FIRST

"Seek first His kingdom and His righteousness, and all these things will be provided to you."

MATTHEW 6:33 NASB

Is it possible we are more amenable to adopting the first part of this instruction than the second? Seek first his kingdom. Okay, I'm in. And his righteousness. *Wait, what? I can't just run after God and enjoy all his blessings? I have to pursue righteousness?*

Are we really so surprised? What we're after is the contentment of the Lord. Did we really think we could find it without also pursuing a life that looks like his? As is always the case, his commands to us are for us. Righteousness, or right living, is living in love, truth, and peace. Doesn't that sound exactly like the kind of place contentment would be found?

Following righteousness will lead to God. Ask him to help you live righteously, that you might find all you need.

NO SHOW

"When you pray, don't be like the hypocrites who love to pray publicly on street corners and in the synagogues where everyone can see them. I tell you the truth, that is all the reward they will ever get."

MATTHEW 6:5 NLT

Prayers are directed toward God not others. You might have heard others pray in a group or a church setting and they seem so good at it. But prayer is not a skill. It is communicating: an open dialogue with the Creator.

It doesn't matter how the words sound to other people; it matters what your heart is really saying, and it is only God who knows your heart. So, don't put your words on display; simply talk with God and share your needs and the needs of others with him.

Ask someone how you can pray for them today. Spend some time in open communication with the Father.

DON'T LOSE HEART

Don't allow yourselves to be weary in planting good seeds, for the season of reaping the wonderful harvest you've planted is coming!

GALATIANS 6:9 TPT

Most fruit trees take at least five years to produce a good harvest of fruit. For the first four years, tending a brand-new orchard is bound to be a little disheartening at times. Will all the effort pay off?

So too in our faith life, long seasons of sowing, tending, and waiting can pick away at our peace. Remember every step is progress, even well before the first bloom. The seeds must be planted, the trunk must grow tall and the branches strong before the apple blooms, so keep planting and take heart.

God does not grow tired waiting for you to bloom, to bear fruit. Take heart from his patient strength and willing waiting, and keep sowing seeds. Tend the branches, water the roots, and trust that one day, there will be fruit.

ON MY SIDE

He is my rock and my salvation;
he is my fortress, I will never be shaken.

Psalm 62:2 NIV

Worry is faith going in the opposite direction. Faith is expecting God to be true to his promises and to act in line with his character. Worry expects the worst. The psalmist makes it pretty clear that worry is not beneficial to us; he describes it as paralyzing. When worry sticks our feet to the ground and makes us gaze more at ourselves than at Christ, when troubles replay over in our heads and make us unable to act, we need to remember where our help comes from.

God has a great track record. He is always good, he always shows up, and he always comes through. He is perfectly just and abundantly righteous. He knows what is best for you; he will never leave you.

Don't let fear make you live your Christian life crippled. Cry out to God for more faith; stand up and walk in the promises he has given you.

SHARED FEELINGS

Trust in the LORD always,
for the LORD GOD is the eternal Rock.

ISAIAH 26:4 NLT

Are you someone who likes to verbally process your thoughts and feelings, or would you rather keep them to yourself? Do you share more than you listen, or listen more than you share? Either way, it is important to make sure you do both. Hopefully you know the people in your life that you can fully trust. If they have faith like you, they will be people that you can collectively speak to God with.

You might have joys; you might have concerns. Share them all, and share them together, because God will help you. Don't forget that after you bring your heart to God, you need to give yourself time to simply pause in his presence.

Take time to pause in God's presence. Thank him for those around you with whom you can share your joys and concerns.

THIRSTY SOUL

You, God, are my God, earnestly I seek you;
I thirst for you, my whole being longs for you,
in a dry and parched land
where there is no water.

Psalm 63:1 NIV

There are times when we feel pretty dry on the inside. You might have felt distant from God for a long time or maybe it has even felt like he has been distant from you. Think back to a time when you were really passionate for Jesus, and you seemed to be getting so much out of Scripture, worship, and prayer times.

Life has its seasons and so does your journey with Christ. Instead of thirsting for the old times, thirst for new ones that are waiting for the door of your heart to open.

Let God into your heart again and give him the opportunity to do something fresh and new. He is near near and ready to breathe something new into your life.

FOUNDED ON FAITH

"The rain descended, the floods came, and the winds blew and beat on that house; and it did not fall, for it was founded on the rock."

MATTHEW 7:25 NKJV

Life's most difficult situations are often compared to storms. Considering the passage above, it's easy to see why. Issues pour upon us, calamities rise around us, and problems beat against us, sometimes all at once. These tough times are often when our faith is tested. When we face disaster, we learn how solid our foundation is. Relying on our own strength—or counting on others to be our source of stability—we may find ourselves flattened once the clouds recede.

A life founded on faith in God, built according to his Word, and assembled with his truth is solid and able to withstand even the strongest of storms. We may find ourselves battered, but we will be standing. With Christ as our foundation, strong and certain, we remain upright.

Build your life on Jesus. His Word is your cornerstone and his sacrifice and grace your pillars. When you are founded in him, you can't be toppled.

FLOWING RIVERS

"He who believes in Me, as the Scripture has said, out of his heart will flow rivers of living water."

JOHN 7:38 NKJV

Water is crucial to human life. Did you know that 70% of our world is covered by water? Even more fascinating, only 1% of that is drinkable by humans. Did you know that our bodies are made up of almost 60% water? Think about this. There is water all around us, but so little of it can give us life and will quench our thirst.

Spiritually, there are options abounding in our world. But only Jesus will quench the thirst of the world. You know the living water himself. You believe in Jesus. Out of you can flow rivers of living water for a thirsty world. How are you taking the gospel to the world? Those who don't know Jesus are swimming in the 70%, and they are so thirsty. You have access to the 1% of life-giving, drinkable water that they need. What are you going to do about it? Fellow believer, share the gospel!

Think of who you can offer living water to today and let it flow from your heart to theirs.

SOURCE OF HOPE

You are my hope;
Lord God, You are my confidence from my youth.

Psalm 71:5 NASB

What does it really mean that God is our hope? Hope is considered one of the primary virtues of Christianity, along with faith and love. Without hope, however, the other two cease. God is the origin of our hope. It comes from him. Jesus is the reason for our hope. He died on the cross and saved us from our sins. The Holy Spirit is the source of our hope. The Holy Spirit is where we draw our hope from.

If something is not found in and powered by God, it can do us no good. This may seem like circular reasoning, but it is so beautiful because with God being the origin, reason, and source of our hope, none of that is worked out in our own strength! The pressure is off us and on God.

God will never fail; he is faithful to deliver. If concepts like hope, love, and faith seem abstract to you, find a way to make them practical today.

WE CANNOT LOSE

Even in the midst of all these things, we triumph over them all, for God has made us to be more than conquerors, and his demonstrated love is our glorious victory over everything.

ROMANS 8:37 TPT

Who doesn't love an underdog? There's something about the unlikely victory of a come-from-behind triumph that reminds us with faith, anything is possible. We may even feel like the underdog sometimes. We may feel hopelessly week or outmatched but don't despair. Take comfort knowing we cannot lose because God has made us conquerors and promised us glorious victory.

Remember, our promise in Christ is not that we won't struggle, but that we won't be defeated. In the midst of it all, because of his great love, the hard-won battle is ours.

By letting you face a powerful opponent, God can show you how truly powerful he is, and how unstoppable you are with him.

THE WHOLE THING

"Be wholeheartedly devoted to the Lord our God to walk in his statutes and to keep his commands, as it is today."

1 Kings 8:61 CSB

Can you kind of lie? Can you be a little bit married? Sort of pregnant? Neither can you be somewhat devoted to the Lord. The truth is, we are either following him, or we are not. We can't worship Christ on Sunday and around our Christian friends, and then forget him on Friday night at an after-work happy hour.

This doesn't mean we can't and won't make mistakes. The Lord loves our obedient actions, but what he requires is our dedicated hearts. Just as a half-truth is not the truth, a partially surrendered heart is not what Jesus wants from you. He wants your whole heart.

You can honor Jesus' sacrifice by giving him your whole heart. Walk in his statutes and keep his commandments, and you will find your devotion increasing.

FAMILY HISTORY

I will sing of the steadfast love of the LORD, forever;
with my mouth I will make known your faithfulness to all generations.

PSALM 89:1 NIV

If you think back through your family history, where did the message of Jesus start? You might have a long history of believers, or you might be the first one in your family to believe. Either way, God allows his message to transfer throughout the generations.

Thank the Lord that you have either been part of a long heritage of faith, or that you are the very first fresh beginning of a faith that will go beyond you. The steadfast love of God will be passed on to future generations as you share your faith.

Remember that you are a significant part of passing on the truth of the gospel. Don't shy away from it! Sing of his steadfast love!

HE WON'T FORGET

He will not forget the needs of the poor.
One day the needy will be remembered,
and their hopes will not be forever dashed in disappointment.

PSALM 9:18 TPT

Loneliness plagues this generation that is supposed to be more connected than ever before. With so many opportunities for instant human interaction, why is loneliness an issue? Our souls were made to be in union with God. When we aren't in relationship with him, our human connections can only sustain us so much. Our priorities are out of line when we rely on those around us to cure us of the deep loneliness in our souls.

It is not anyone else's job to meet your need for loneliness. That can only be met in Christ. When loneliness arises in you, let it be the red flag that sends you running to God. Don't try to fulfill those needs in other manners with other things. Pay attention to your soul and find refuge in God alone.

You will never be forgotten by God. He will not leave you alone. Have faith in his patience, mercy, and staying power.

PRAYER OF FAITH

"If you can?" said Jesus. "Everything is possible for one who believes."

Mark 9:23 NIV

When you pray, are you doing it in a spirit of boldness, expecting that God can change the circumstance? Sometimes it's as if we are afraid to bother God with our requests, so we speak tentatively, "Dear Lord, if it is your will, it'd be great if you could..." "Father, I know you have so many bigger things, but I'd love it if...."

Let's stop with faithless prayers. God knows your heart already. Believe that he can do what you are asking. There is no need for caution with the Father who loves you so dearly.

Approach God's throne of grace with boldness and ask that he make things possible because of your faith in him.

HELD TOGETHER

He's the hope that holds me
and the Stronghold to shelter me,
the only God for me, and my great confidence.

Psalm 91:2 TPT

There are many things you can place your hope in that will let you down. We tend to do it often. We place our hope in political candidates, our career, our spouses, our health, our financial status, our achievements or accolades, our presence on social media, our friendships; the general list could go on and on, and each of us could probably write our own specific list as well.

Not all of these are bad things to hope in or for. God is not upset at you if you hope to get that promotion, be married, or desire to have friendships. The difference lies in lining up your life with hope that cannot be shaken.

Your first and most prominent hope should be in Jesus. That hope can never disappoint. From this hope, all other hopes flow.

FULLY TRUST GOD

Trust in the Lord with all your heart,
And lean not on your own understanding.

Proverbs 3:5 NKJV

Trust can be hard to put into action mostly because our experience with others tells us that we can be sorely disappointed. People let us down in many ways. We can even be disappointed in ourselves. Remember the trust game that involved standing with eyes closed and falling back into the hands of a few peers in hopes that they would catch you? There was risk involved in that game, and it didn't always turn out well. Nothing can truly be guaranteed in this life, can it? Well, it depends on where you place your trust.

God watches over us, cares for us, and is involved in our lives. When we acknowledge that every good thing comes from him, our faith is strengthened and we are able to trust him more.

Make a point of noticing how God directs your paths today, and thank him for being trustworthy.

STEP OUT IN FAITH

Tell the priests who carry the ark of the covenant: "When you reach the edge of the Jordan's waters, go and stand in the river."

JOSHUA 3:7-8 NIV

God often doesn't show us the entire plan when he calls us to do something. Joshua and the Israelites had to cross the Jordan River before they could enter the Promised Land. God told Joshua that he would part the waters for them. The priests, leading the way with the ark, walked into the water first. There stood the priests—partially immersed in water—waiting for God to do what he said he would.

It must have taken great faith to stand in the water, waiting for the miracle to happen. Sometimes God will have us walk right into a river before he parts the water because the work he can do in our hearts with a simple act of faith is well worth our temporary fear.

If God were to show you the step-by-step plan, then faith wouldn't be necessary. God knows what your humanity can handle, and in light of that, he won't share with you what you don't need to know.

MYSTERY AND HOPE

Since through God's mercy we have this ministry, we do not lose heart. Rather, we have renounced secret and shameful ways; we do not use deception, nor do we distort the word of God. On the contrary, by setting forth the truth plainly we commend ourselves to everyone's conscience in the sight of God.

2 Corinthians 4:1-2 NIV

There is so much mystery to life. So many unanswered questions and unknowns. Faith in and of itself is a huge element of mystery. In order to live a faith-filled life, we accept the elements of mystery because we know what goes hand-in-hand with it—hope.

Hope is God telling us that his purpose is bigger than any unknown. When we walk through anything, no matter how great a mystery, God is walking alongside us. He doesn't promise us an explanation, and therein lies the mystery. But he does promise his presence, and that is an unfailing truth. When we walk through deep waters, he is there.

When you experience an unexplained circumstance or situation that you wish you could ask God about, know deep in your heart that hope is waiting on the other side of the mystery.

BRAVE BELIEF

"Truly, truly, I say to you, whoever believes in me will also do the works that I do; and greater works than these will he do, because I am going to the Father. Whatever you ask in my name, this I will do, that the Father may be glorified in the Son. If you ask me anything in my name, I will do it."

JOHN 14:12-14 ESV

One of the bravest, most courageous things we can do as children of God is simply to believe him at his word. He takes great delight when his children trust that all his promises are good and true.

Today, refuse cynicism, skepticism, and arrogance and instead courageously say to the Father, "I will trust you and, by faith, ask great things in your name."

Have you resisted through doubt something God has asked you to believe him for? Start trusting him for it today.

OUT OF THE PIT

You brought me up from the grave, O LORD.
You kept me from falling into the pit of death.

PSALM 30:3 NLT

It is hard to understand how and when God heals his children. Have you prayed for healing recently and haven't got any better? Do you know someone around you that is unwell and not recovering?

It can be disheartening when you are sick or see others that you care about not improving. Our faith does not need to be great, but through our belief in Jesus we can also acknowledge our belief in the miracles that he performed. Jesus showed us that what we think is impossible is not impossible with God.

Continue to pray for healing in your life and in the life of those around you. Jesus has compassion to heal, but sometimes he doesn't answer exactly how you want. Trust that he is always good, no matter what.

IN CHARGE

"I am not even worthy to come and meet you. Just say the word from where you are, and my servant will be healed."

LUKE 7:7 NLT

Most of us like to think we're in control of situations. We often think we are more relaxed when we're in control. But no matter how good it feels to be in charge, there are times when we are relieved to give it up. We realize how much we can't control. Nothing brings that into reality as forcefully as sickness—ours—or someone we love.

In the same way the centurion gave orders and was obeyed, he believed Jesus' authority could cure his servant's illness. He understood the power of Jesus' command. We often spin our wheels trying to make things turn out the way we think they should. If you have been labeled a control freak, you know how hard it is to let go. Relinquishing control can be gut-wrenching. But it can also be a huge relief and a giant leap toward rest.

Authority is an amazing thing. When you submit to Jesus, it takes the weighty yoke of control from you. You will find relief and rest because the one in command is worthy of all authority and he has your best in mind.

A DESCRIPTION OF GLORY

Above this surface was something that looked like a throne made of blue lapis lazuli. And on this throne high above was a figure whose appearance resembled a man. From what appeared to be his waist up, he looked like gleaming amber, flickering like a fire. And from his waist down, he looked like a burning flame, shining with splendor.

Ezekiel 1:26-27 NLT

When we think of Jesus, we are familiar with the descriptions given in the gospels—a man just like us who was born and raised as a Jew and walked with ordinary people. When we hear of Jesus having descended from glory and then being raised again to glory, we begin to get a glimpse of this glorified Jesus with the vision that Ezekiel had.

Human words can only begin to describe the magnificence of Christ. We serve a risen Lord who is now on the throne and he is as consuming and beautiful as an amber flame, ready to shine through your life today.

Although he humbled himself to become like us on earth, Jesus also defeated death and now stands victorious. Choose to be encouraged by your future with him in glory as you go into your day.

A LITTLE WOBBLY

Direct my footsteps according to your word;
let no sin rule over me.

Psalm 119:133 NIV

Family albums often boast a picture of a young girl in her mama's high heels, tiny feet barely making it past the arch, stubby legs only slightly longer than the shoes. What is it about those shoes that, even as little girls, make women feel beautiful? They're certainly not comfortable or easy to move in, but women want to feel elegant and those narrow, pointy pumps have a way of bringing out their inner princess. Whether worn daily or saved for special occasions, chances are those heels make steps a little wobbly at times.

Stepping out in faith is similar. Getting used to walking in faith, we're a little shaky and uncertain. People with more faith seem to be everywhere, and they make it look so much more graceful than we feel. But that beautifully coiffed woman in the stilettos? She's teetering too. This is one of many reasons we need the Holy Spirit. The Helper is a strong, steady arm, directing our steps, keeping us steady in the Word, and steering us away from sin.

Walking in faith isn't always easy or without pain. Thank God for being your steady hand who holds you up.

ALLOWED TO ENTER

Yahweh, who dares to dwell with you?
Who presumes the privilege of being close to you,
living next to you in your shining place of glory?

PSALM 15:1 TPT

The thought of someone unclean being able to meet with Jesus without any formal ceremony would have been entirely offensive to the Israelites. Our ability to simply ask for forgiveness and expect to feel God's presence within us would have been daring and presumptuous.

Have you felt God's presence lately? Take a moment to appreciate the transforming power of the cross that enabled you to live right next to the shining glory of God and daily dwell in the life of the Holy Spirit.

You are seen as blameless and pure even though you may not see yourself that way. You are likely aware of your unworthiness. Keep reminding yourself that you are worthy because Jesus has made you worthy.

JUNE

I took my troubles to the LORD;
I cried out to him,
and he answered my prayer.

PSALM 120:1 NLT

EFFICIENTLY

Having such a hope, we use great boldness in our speech.

2 CORINTHIANS 3:12 NASB

Have you ever known someone who communicates efficiently and bluntly? They do not mince words, and if not presented with tact, their words can wound or cause offense. Maybe you are seeking counsel. It is in your interest for that person to transfer information truthfully, but also with compassion.

In carrying out the great commission, we have a responsibility to present our faith accurately and courageously in love. We must know the Word and present the gospel unapologetically, proving that we are faithful followers who are not ashamed of the gospel. We may witness to people who will hear about Jesus from no one else. If we had the cure for cancer, we wouldn't bury it. Why do we hesitate to tell others of the greatest hope there is?

Do you worry about what others think of your faith? Be brave in sharing the gift of God that leads to redemption.

FOR THE RUN

Not that I have already obtained this or am already perfect, but I press on to make it my own, because Christ Jesus has made me his own.

PHILIPPIANS 3:12 ESV

You likely don't remember the day, but do you recall the general time you realized you had stopped growing? Your pants stopped getting too short; your shoes stopped getting too tight. For women, the shoe thing is kind of a thrill. These will still fit next summer? Let the collection commence!

Shortly after we stopped growing physically, we realized how very far we still had to grow. True friendships deepened, while others faded away. The more complicated our choices became, the easier it was to see who believed as we did and valued what we valued. Whether eighteen or eighty, if we are growing in Christ, the process continues to this day. It never really ends.

Strive for perfection not because you need to earn God's love or you're in competition with someone else; do it because becoming better means becoming more like God.

PERFECTION

Since you are waiting for these, be diligent to be found by him without spot or blemish, and at peace.

2 PETER 3:14 ESV

It seems unreasonable to ask us to be spotless, considering we make mistakes every day. Remember that Jesus took your place so you will be found without blemish. It is not about living a perfect life, it is about knowing and believing that he has made you perfect.

Jesus' blood has washed away every sin. You are forgiven and made new. Continue to put your trust and faith in Jesus, knowing that one day your wait for full perfection will be over.

Stop striving for perfection and instead receive it by God's grace.

BOUND TOGETHER

Above all, clothe yourselves with love, which binds us all together in perfect harmony.

COLOSSIANS 3:14 NLT

Do you sometimes question the way the church is set up, how it functions, and what its purpose is? As we face all kinds of uncertainty, including the ability for governments to stop us from meeting together in our faith gatherings, it does us good to think about things we often take for granted.

You might have felt obligated to go to church or a Bible study, but when the occurrences of the outside world stop you from doing those, you realize how truly precious hanging out with other believers is. Aside from your thoughts on worship, sermons, and volunteering at church, can you see that it really is love that keeps us together?

Pursue being with other believers simply because it is a way to share in the love that God has so freely given to you.

PROVIDING AN ANSWER

In your hearts revere Christ as Lord. Always be prepared to give an answer to everyone who asks you to give the reason for the hope that you have. But do this with gentleness and respect.

1 PETER 3:15 NIV

Peter told his readers not to be afraid to suffer for doing what was right. He said that if we insist on obeying God, our suffering would bring blessing. Instead of fearing threats, he said we ought to revere Christ in our hearts. In other words, we should honor him and serve him above all. If he really is Lord of our lives, then his eternal glory will matter more to us than our temporary suffering.

When we have this mindset, it will change the way we face challenges and act in difficult times. The hope that we have in Christ will be evident. Someone may ask where our strength and our joy come from. We can respectfully reply that our hope is found in Christ alone.

Let God fill you with hope and set you apart from the dizziness of the world. When others ask how you maintain your joy and focus, trust God to give you the right words to say with a gentle delivery.

ALL YOU ASK

This is how we have come to know love: He laid down his life for us. We should also lay down our lives for our brothers and sisters.

1 John 3:16 csb

May we never lose our amazement about this: Jesus gave up his life for us. And may we never grow unimpressed by those who take up the noble charge of sharing their faith. All around the world are brothers and sisters willing to set everything aside to bring this incredible truth to those who haven't heard it.

In many countries, evangelism is a crime. Christians sit in jail because they were caught saying Jesus' name, telling others what he did for them. May we not be unmoved to pray for their provision, protection, and peace.

From the safety and comfort of your home, lay down your concerns today and pray for people who are sharing their faith in the face of persecution. Pray they would be protected, provided for, and filled with peace.

IN THE STORY

If anyone has the world's goods and sees his brother in need, yet closes his heart against him, how does God's love abide in him?

1 John 3:17 ESV

Have you had the experience of reading a really good book, or watching a great movie, and then thinking about it all day almost as if you were one of the characters or like the plot actually happened to you? Stories can be all-consuming, so why not let the story of Christ consume your heart today?

Find some time to read a chapter or watch a Bible story and then put yourself in that story. Let yourself hear Jesus as if he were speaking directly to you. Imagine yourself watching the others around you as they hear Jesus. Imagine seeing one of your friends being healed. You are in the story of Christ whether it is written down or not. Be Jesus to those around you.

As you place yourself in this story of our faith, let the love of Jesus spill out into your actions for others.

LUKEWARM

"You say, 'I'm rich, I have become wealthy and need nothing,' and you don't realize that you are wretched, pitiful, poor, blind, and naked."

REVELATION 3:17 CSB

Being comfortable is nice, but it can also lead you into a place of laziness. You know what it is like when you find that nice warm spot in a big comfortable chair at the end of the night–it makes you want to sleep.

Remember that we can't get too comfortable with our faith. We need to experience a certain amount of tension, so we can stay committed to the cause of sharing Christ with a world that desperately needs him.

Ask Jesus to restore your passion to see him working in the world. You can be used by him if you'll give him your time and your talent.

A BLAZING FURNACE

"Even if he does not, we want you to know, Your Majesty, that we will not serve your gods or worship the image of gold you have set up."

DANIEL 3:18 NIV

Would we be willing to risk our lives so as not to compromise God's truth? We would like to think that we would be brave enough, but it would be the hardest thing we would ever have to do.

Thankfully, most of us aren't put through a life-and-death situation when it comes to speaking God's truth, but our faith should be just as strong nonetheless. The Holy Spirit is with us all throughout the day; we can draw from the power and strength that he so freely gives.

Surprise yourself with the boldness that comes from knowing you serve the one and only living God. When people or situations challenge your faith, ask for a renewed vigor to defend what you know is true.

CONFIDENT IN HOPE

We are confident of all this because of our great trust in God through Christ.

2 Corinthians 3:4 NLT

Side by side are two runners. Thirteen miles ahead is a finish line. Runner number one has been training for weeks, following a schedule geared toward getting her to the finish line. Because she's prepared, she feels ready and excited for the run. Runner number two hasn't run more than a few blocks in five years, but she ran track in high school, and she knows a lot of people who have run half-marathons. She figures if they can do it, she can too. Both are confident, but one with more reason.

While ambition is an admirable quality, the confidence you gain from a disciplined life surrendered to Christ is something you can take straight to the altar of God. How would you rate your overall confidence? Do you find yourself feeling stronger and more assured in some aspects of life than others? Turning specifically to your faith, how strong, truly, is your confidence in God? Do you believe he hears your prayers, and that he is always for you?

Reflect on the times God has worked good in your life, and let your confidence soar.

UNTIL WE KNOW

The Lord is not slow in doing what he promised—the way some people understand slowness. But God is being patient with you. He does not want anyone to be lost, but he wants all people to change their hearts and lives.

2 Peter 3:9 NCV

What if God decided that today was the day he's coming back? How many souls would be lost, whether out of rebellion or ignorance? If eternity started today, would you spend it without someone who matters to you?

How wonderful it is to know we have a patient, loving God! Because he loves us, he wants to make sure that we who belong to him have time to share his heart, and that those who don't yet know it will realize they too are his.

Your future is secure; you will be with Jesus in heaven. Are there people you love who have not yet accepted the incredible gift of his grace? Pray for their salvation today.

LONELINESS

The LORD watches over those who fear him,
those who rely on his unfailing love.

PSALM 33:18 NLT

Loneliness can drive us one of two ways. It can either take us closer to God or further from him. When our hearts are in despair, we tend to want to isolate even further. We must not give in, allowing the lie of God's indifference to win. Let loneliness drive you to God.

When you feel abandoned by others, tell God about it. He is near; the Bible promises that. If the Bible says it's true, then everything else is a lie. Stand on the promise of Scripture today and draw near to God.

When you are feeling lonely, turn your face toward God. Run into his open arms. His words are solid and true. He is always near, and his eyes are on you. Choose to believe it.

SURE FOUNDATION

He will be the sure foundation for your times,
a rich store of salvation and wisdom and knowledge;
the fear of the LORD is the key to this treasure.

ISAIAH 33:6 NIV

We wouldn't expect a house of cards built on something soft like a pillow to be very tall or stand for very long. A granite countertop provides a much better foundation. Even a jigsaw puzzle wouldn't hold up very well on the softer surface. We need something solid beneath the things we build.

When it comes to our lives, the principle is the same. Building on our faith in the Lord, we can expect safety. If we piece our future together based on respect for him, wisdom and knowledge will be ours.

God is your firm foundation. When you stand on his wisdom, you will be strong. Relying on his knowledge, you can be sure. When you respect God the way he deserves, your house will go up safe, sturdy, and tall.

CHOOSING PRAISE

I will glory in the LORD; let the afflicted hear and rejoice. Glorify the LORD with me; let us exalt his name together.

PSALM 34:2-3 NIV

Do we only praise God for something after he has given it, or do we praise him ahead of time in faith, knowing that he will always be good no matter what happens? We should look at difficulties in life as miracles waiting to happen, as chances for God to show his goodness and bring us closer to his heart.

Sometimes it is difficult to praise God. We don't see him in our lives or in others' the way we would like to. News of the day can be depressing. But we can choose praise. And we can make that choice every moment of the day.

Can you choose praise today? The world is discouraging, but God is not. Remember that as you offer him your honor and gratitude.

GET BACK UP

The LORD directs the steps of the godly.
He delights in every detail of their lives.
Though they stumble, they will never fall,
for the LORD holds them by the hand.

PSALM 37:23-24 NLT

We cling to all the verses in the Bible about God being with us, prospering our ways, lifting us up. This verse is one of them. But a little section we often pass by: *though they stumble*. It doesn't say if, or maybe. It says that they will.

Too often we think we should never fail. If we have failed, or stumbled, things must not be going right. We maybe even think that because we fail at something God is not with us. Here, the Psalmist almost guarantees us that we will fail. But failure is not the end. Steps of faith and acts of bravery are often paired with failure. It is a trap for us to believe that we shouldn't fail. That trap makes us not want to get back up, try again, or step out in faith. Read the rest of the passage. Who is holding your hand? Who is directing your steps? Who is taking pleasure in the details of your life? Jesus.

Though you fail, God is with you. Get up and take another leap of faith today.

MY LIVING HOPE

Blessed be the God and Father of our Lord Jesus Christ, who according to His great mercy has caused us to be born again to a living hope through the resurrection of Jesus Christ from the dead.

1 Peter 1:3 NASB

Have you heard of the term *false hope*? False hope refers to having confidence in something that is not true. It is based on ignorance. How can you be sure that your faith in Christ is not just false hope? Has the fear ever arisen that you are dedicating your life to a lost cause? If so, quiet those fears with fact. The hope you have in Christ is based on the character of God and the work of Jesus. He died for your sins, overcame death, and rose from the dead. He is alive today; he is your living hope.

It is not just wishful thinking or false hope because it is backed by the entire character of God. Your salvation is sealed by God himself. Throw your life into living for Jesus; it's not a lost cause but a sure and living hope—one you can bet your life on.

Be encouraged! Jesus is your living hope.

GOODNESS OF GOD

Because you have these blessings, do your best to add these things to your lives: to your faith, add goodness; and to your goodness, add knowledge.

2 Peter 1:5 NCV

What would it look like to add goodness to our faith? In Greek, the word for *goodness* can also be translated as virtue, uprightness, or a gracious act. Perhaps goodness is our faith in action. Just as the book of James advises us that faith without works is dead, how we live our faith is a representation of the beliefs we hold. If we claim to believe that God is faithful, that he is full of compassion, and that he is for us, then our lives and actions will align with those beliefs.

This is not to say that we need to be perfect in faith. Christ alone perfects us. We are covered in his faithfulness even when we are faithless. For those who want to live surrendered to Christ, we get to continually humble ourselves before him. We can seek to represent his truth in the choices we make, both big and small.

How can you intentionally live out your faith in Jesus? Continually thank him for his goodness and reflect his love to others.

PERSIST

Our hope for you is firmly grounded, knowing that as you are partners in our sufferings, so also you are in our comfort.

2 CORINTHIANS 1:7 NASB

The three women really wanted a service project where they could work together for the good of others. They prayed about an opportunity, and God in his faithfulness answered. There was an older couple that desperately needed help with just about everything. Eventually, the needs of the elderly people got a bit overwhelming. Two of the women got tired of the constant requests and felt they had to bow out. The remaining woman decided to stick with it, and her relationship with the older couple deepened. She ended up getting far more out of the friendship than she felt she put in.

We can get weary of praying the same request for years. Waiting for someone we are discipling to really commit to giving Jesus control of their lives can be discouraging. Some days we just want to throw in the towel. If we believe Scripture, we will soldier on. God promises that if we persist, we'll see the evidence of our faith. It might be hard and exhausting, but if we're doing it to serve Christ, it will be worth it.

Don't give up! Stay the course and see what God will do.

WHEREVER YOU GO

Have I not commanded you? Be strong and courageous. Do not be afraid; do not be discouraged, for the LORD your God will be with you wherever you go.

JOSHUA 1:9 NIV

After Moses died, the Lord commanded Joshua to cross over the Jordan River and possess the land. He reassured Joshua that there was nothing to be afraid of because he would go with him. Was it not, after all, God who commanded him to do so? Joshua listened to the voice of God, and he used God's Word as a guide, not turning to either the right or the left.

When God calls us to something, he will also provide a way. Our part is to simply follow him in faith. The more our faith is tested and God proves his loyalty, the more confident we become. Rather than allow obstacles to discourage us, we can be encouraged knowing that God goes with us wherever we go.

Go is all-sufficient and all-powerful. Whatever he leads you to, he will also lead you through. Have faith and follow him!

SO FAR AWAY

Lord, why do you seem so far away when evil is near?
Why have you hidden yourself when I need you the most?

PSALM 10:1 TPT

Can you think of those times when you want to yell and shout at God that he doesn't care? Today might be one of those days, or perhaps you have been feeling this way for longer—like months or maybe even years. We have periods of feeling like God is completely absent, possibly to the point of questioning our faith.

Don't feel alone with thoughts like these; God can handle it. In those times where it feels like God is hiding, allow yourself to pursue him and use it as an opportunity to seek him until you do find him.

When it feels like God is absent, become the pursuer and seek him out. You will find him if you look for him.

POWER OF KINDNESS

You gave me life and faithful love,
and your care has guarded my life.

Job 10:12 CSB

A person with great tolerance is said to have the patience of Job. Someone enduring a horrible string of circumstances may say they feel like Job. Most adults are familiar with at least the basics of Job's story: he's the one who lost everything—his wealth, his children, and his health, and yet stayed faithful to God.

Oh, that we would feel like Job! Look at these beautiful words again, and consider the speaker. His children have all died. His home and his wealth have been wiped away. His body is in constant agony, and none of his friends are standing by him. By many standards, he had indeed lost everything. But look at what he still had. The things that sustained him are things that could not be taken away.

There is incredible joy to be found in suffering. Stay close to God in your times of trouble and you will experience part of what Job did.

LISTEN IN THE DARK

"What I say to you in the dark, repeat in broad daylight, and what you hear in a whisper, announce it publicly."

MATTHEW 10:27 TPT

When it's dark, our other senses become keener to compensate for the lack of light. We make ourselves still to hear the whisper of a loved one, and it almost feels easier than if you could see them. We are focused on the voice. We should hear the whispers of God so clearly in the dark that we can shout it from rooftops when morning dawns.

What we hear we are supposed to share. Dark seasons are not wasted. Jesus is speaking to you, advocating for you, and building you up, just like in the light. When you reach morning, he wants you to tell others who may be in the dark the things he spoke to you. He wants you to shout and share. Isn't it beautiful that with God, no season is wasted? Tune your ear to hear in the darkness and start to make known what was entrusted to you.

Thank God that he is ever near. Your happy life is dependent solely on being close to him. He will speak in the dark times and the light, and he wastes nothing in your life.

GOOD NEWS

"Whoever believes in Him will not be put to shame."

ROMANS 10:11 NASB

Confession. Most people don't get warm fuzzies from the word, understandably. In every other case, for something to be confessed implies wrongness: wrong actions, wrong motives, wrong us. We confess to committing a crime, to cheating on a test, to betraying a confidence. We don't confess to getting a promotion, getting engaged, or joining a new Bible study.

But a confession of faith is different. What we're professing is our admission into God's family, and there's certainly nothing wrong with that. Confessing Jesus died for us and believing that he was raised from the dead is enough to set us right with him.

Confess your faith again today. Consider it a gift and a source of freedom.

SATISFIED HUNGER

He satisfies the longing soul,
and the hungry soul he fills with good things.

Psalm 107:9 ESV

The appetite is a funny thing. Our bodies have the ability to communicate hunger to our brains, and our brains then cause us to seek out a solution to the problem. When we are genuinely hungry, we look for food that will fill our stomachs and quiet our hunger.

Our souls have appetites also, but we so easily spend our time and energy on the world's entertainment. We fill ourselves up with things that will never be able to satisfy and leave little room for the only one who can.

Watch what you fill your soul with today. Feast on the goodness of God so you don't remain hungry.

TAKE THAT LEAP

We have this hope as an anchor for the soul, firm and secure.

HEBREWS 6:19 NIV

We all have hopes, dreams, and plans. Many of us feel as though the dreams have been buried. Some dreams may be on hold because the timing is not right yet. You may have bigger hopes, such as a family member's salvation or a better career, or smaller hopes like surviving a rough patch or being able to take a break.

Hope is a great motivator, but we need to be able to move to faith. Faith is the tangible outworking of our hope. It is that first step. It's the little kid jumping into a mud puddle, knowing his boots will keep him warm. Faith is saying yes to things that move us forward and letting go of the fear or circumstance that hold us back. Sometimes faith can be waiting patiently for the right timing. When that time comes, put your hope into action!

God wants to move and work in your life, and he wants to fulfil the dreams that have come from him. Take the leap, land in the puddle, and you will find yourself dancing in the rain.

FAITH WINS

By this our ancestors were approved.

HEBREWS 11:2 CSB

Most people will go to extravagant extremes to win approval. Achieve more, learn more, do more, succeed more, over and over again in hopes of receiving the praise they desire. It's a never-ending, exhausting cycle of finding new ways to gain the applause of others.

Our spiritual forefathers had one step to receiving approval—faith. The patriarchs walked with God daily, nurturing a deep personal relationship with the Father. This closeness with the Father resulted in great faith which he counted as righteousness, and he was pleased by their unwavering trust. The only approval we need is from our Creator, and the way to win it is faith in him, pure and simple.

Ask God for the gift of faith so you can please him. Trust in him instead of yourself, and you will receive his approval.

FAITH IN ACTION

"Even more blessed are all who hear the word of God and put it into practice."

LUKE 11:28 NLT

In relationships, our words only count for so much if they are not backed up with action. It is the same in our relationship with God. Where we find ourselves in agreement with the Word of God in what we say, think, or believe, let us be people who live these things out in practical ways, practicing what we proclaim.

Consider the last time you gave someone a piece of advice. Was it something you believed to be true? Is it also something that you have been living? Sometimes truth becomes such a part of our psyches that we can easily spout off answers. However, it doesn't always show up as easily in the choices we make. Let's be people who put our faith into action.

Ask for eyes to see where your life is not aligned with God's truth. Be empowered by his Spirit to live the truth of his radical love in every area.

GIVE THANKS

Give thanks to the LORD, for he is good;
his love endures forever.

PSALM 118:1 NIV

Psalm 118 was written during unbelievable devastation. Conditions were not good. David was in the middle of terrible times, with enemies encamped on every side, when he called out to God. He said he felt pushed back and about to fall. But even in this seemingly impossible scenario, he put his trust in God's faithfulness to protect him.

To emphasize the faith the Psalmist had in God, he began and ended the chapter with the same message: give thanks to the Lord, for he is good; his love endures forever.

Even during the worst of days, God is still good. His love endures every onslaught and will continue to last forever. Give him thanks for that today.

SUSTAINED BY LOVE

Sustain me according to Your word, that I may live;
And do not let me be ashamed of my hope.

PSALM 119:116 NASB

When the storms of life toss us around, it can be difficult to find our grounding. *Where is God in this?* We may find it hard to see his goodness at all. But even in the chaos, God is full of peace. His Word calms the wildest tempest and makes the sea like glass.

God's Word is full of light; it is sustenance for those who are hungry. We will not be ashamed of our hope if our hope is in God and his faithfulness. When we wonder whether he is present, let us look into history to see what it reveals about his character. When we look with eyes of faith, we will see him. His goodness is inescapable, and his mercy cannot be exaggerated.

God is the one who holds your life. He keeps you even as you stumble.Let him be the strength of your heart and the wisdom you need.

FEAR OF THE DARK

The unfolding of your words gives light;
it gives understanding to the simple.

Psalm 119:130 NASB

The number one fear of most children is darkness. Darkness has an interesting way of making things larger and scarier than they are. It distorts the truth, turning dressers into monsters and curtains into ghosts. It robs you of your ability to see danger, like a Lego looming on the floor in your path. To be people of courage, we need light.

Psalms clearly tells us how to let such light enter our lives—through God's Word. Remove any roadblocks like pride and apathy. Without his Word there is no illumination, and we remain in darkness. Let light expose what seems scary and see that nothing is too big for God. Let light show you danger that is lurking, so you can alter your course. There is no end to the wondrous work that happens in us when we allow light to penetrate every nook of our heart.

Ask God to show you areas of your heart that are dark. Keep his Word ever close and walk as a child of the light.

JULY

"Nothing will be impossible with God."

LUKE 1:37 NASB

THE FIRST THING

I rise before dawn and cry out for help;
I put my hope in your word.

Psalm 119:147 CSB

For a morning person, this verse seems quite reasonable. Whether the sun is up or not, they're awake early and eager to greet the day. For the night owls, rising before the dawn, it sounds, well, like something they would rather not do. They like their sleep. They're comfortable right here between their sheets. Must we all rise before dawn to cry out to God and find our hope?

While Scripture does frequently encourage early rising, it's not so much the hour of the day that matters as the eagerness of the heart. The Psalmist simply cannot wait to get together with God. Regardless of the height of the sun, is time with the Father the first thing on your mind?

Before anyone or anything can distract you, before you've even fully awakened, meet with God. It will set the course for your day.

IN TIMES OF DOUBT

God you are near me always, so close to me;
every one of your commands reveals truth.
I've known all along how true and unchanging
is every word you speak, established forever!

PSALM 119:151-152 TPT

The sun will set tonight; it will rise tomorrow. This is truth. We have no reason to doubt what we've witnessed every day of our lives. But when experience tells us otherwise, or perhaps we have no experience to go on, doubts creep in. It's going to snow tomorrow. "I doubt that," we say.

When someone we trust says they'll be there for us, we have faith in their words. Someone who has repeatedly let us down can make the same promise, but we remain uncertain until they've shown up and proven themselves. We're unsettled. We doubt. God wants to erase our doubt and he will; we only need to have faith.

Examine your prayer life. Do you trust God, or do you doubt his promises to you? Share your heart openly with him, and ask him for unwavering faith.

I LOOK TO YOU

I lift my eyes to you,
the one enthroned in heaven

Psalm 123:1 CSB

When we look expectantly to the Lord, our hearts reach out to his. What do we long for? What do we need? How do we need his mercy and grace to meet us? It is good to recognize where we're at, and it is also necessary to look to God to encounter us with the abundance of his kingdom resources. There is so much more available to us than we realize!

May we offer him the attention of our hearts and get lost in the wonder and beauty of his incomparably good nature. There is no one else like him. Let us lift our eyes from our temporary troubles and fix them on our unchanging Lord, who is glorious in all his ways.

God is far above any trial or trouble you face; his power is overwhelmingly capable of saving you. Don't get lost in the fear of what could come; rather, fix your eyes on him.

BELIEF IN GOD

"Don't worry or surrender to your fear. For you've believed in God, now trust and believe in me also."

JOHN 14:1 TPT

When you get into your car to drive to work, you may flip on the radio and hear some news and the weather. Usually, most of the news is not in your area. A tornado hit a different part of the country, a bank was robbed, or a car accident happened in a different part of the city. Even though you didn't see them happen, you usually believe they did. You also believe the weather person when they say you might need an umbrella later.

We practice belief daily in different ways, but when it comes to belief in God, we often trip up. Fear or doubt creeps in stealthily when it comes to God. Why doesn't it when it comes to the news? We have an enemy whose weapon of fear is used in any way possible to hinder us from belief. Faith is the one requirement of us in Scripture. It makes sense that our enemy would do whatever it takes to destroy that belief.

If you are struggling in your belief of God, cry out to him: "Lord, I believe. Help my unbelief!"

STAY CALM

The LORD himself will fight for you. Just stay calm.

EXODUS 14:14 NLT

The Israelites saw God's miracles and followed him, through Moses, to freedom. Their past captors pursued them. They found themselves cornered and surrounded. Their enemy, determined to destroy them or drag them back into captivity, appeared so mighty. They felt unmatched and hopeless, so they lost faith in the God.

Moses reminded the people that it is the Lord who fights for them, as is always the case with the people of God. We may be no match for our enemies, but they are no match for God. When our bondages seem too tight, or our pasts threaten to drag us back down, or when it seems like an impenetrable force is all around us refusing to let us move forward, we need to turn to God.

Don't get caught up in your own weaknesses or the strength of your enemies. Stand your ground, stay calm, and watch God work on your behalf.

THE WAY

Jesus explained, "I am the Way, I am the Truth, and I am the Life. No one comes next to the Father except through union with me. To know me is to know my Father too."

JOHN 14:6 TPT

"Turn right in 0.5 miles. Your destination is on the left." With the development of GPS, we are used to following the voice, trusting it will get us where we need to go. In fact, studies have shown that the use of GPS is altering our brains. We no longer make mental maps of our surroundings because we aren't paying attention as keenly as we did when we followed an actual map or had to do the navigating ourselves.

While that's not good news for our geographical intelligence, it makes for a great analogy about us and Jesus. Jesus said he is the way. The one way, the only way. Often, we try to navigate the course ourselves, but we have no idea where we are going or how to get there. Jesus has all the information. He knows where the roadblocks are and when construction or weather is going to slow us down.

Jesus is the only way to get to the Father, which is exactly where you need to be. Trust in his voice and leading.

HEARD

LORD, hear my prayer.
In your faithfulness listen to my plea,
and in your righteousness answer me.

PSALM 143:1 CSB

Those who are against the idea of God place their trust in their own judgment of a given circumstance; they rely on their own right-ness. You might have encountered people like this. Thank Jesus you don't have to make those kinds of judgments for yourself.

In the midst of change and decision-making, you have the gift of faith and that will result in a quiet peace in place of worry or self-doubt. God listens. He hears all your questions and concerns when you pour out your heart and mind to him. Be assured that he will answer in his righteousness.

Trust in the God who is real. He truly hears you.

STRETCHED OUT

I stretch out my hands to you;
my soul thirsts for you like a parched land.

PSALM 143:6 ESV

David takes his eyes off his own situation and reflects on the bigger picture. His desire for relief changes to a desire for connection. The temporary external factors momentarily melt away and eternal relationship takes priority.

This is a powerful reminder of a personal God: a God whose first priority is our relational well-being. This is a hard pill to swallow at times, especially if we are suffering. Faith can feel foolish in certain moments. But David says, "I spread out my hands to you," asking God to make sense and meaning out of his circumstances.

Ask God to help bring awareness of his love for you. Feel his embrace in your pain and frustration.

THROUGH FAITH

He brought him outside and said, "Look toward heaven, and number the stars, if you are able to number them." Then he said to him, "So shall your offspring be." And he believed the LORD, and he counted it to him as righteousness.

GENESIS 15:5-6 ESV

This is the famous place in the Bible where we understand that it isn't about what we say or do that saves us, rather, it is what we believe. Abram and Sarah would have undoubtedly felt skeptical that God would give them as many descendants as the stars in the sky as they wrestled with having even one child in their old age.

What God says is truth, and his Word does not come back void. Somewhere along the line, Abram chose to believe and his heart of belief, God said, made him righteous.

As you ponder God's amazing miracle for Abram and Sarah, look for his goodness and truth in your own life.

SWEET RAIN

When the king smiles, there is life;
his favor refreshes like a spring rain.

PROVERBS 16:15 NLT

Rain can be healing. When clouds loom grey and large, we trust in God, and then the rain comes. The rain can wash us clean and change our perspective. Have you ever gone outside after it has rained when the air is crisp and fresh? God can do this with our perspective on hard things as well.

He is the cleansing force we need. We need to be healed by his rain. We need to take the spots of our life that we see as bitter or riddled with clouds and ask him to make them sweet to us. That doesn't necessarily mean he will take the hard things away or change the outcome to what you want, but he will bring goodness out of difficulty. It takes a lot of faith, but God will build up your faith and give you eyes to see.

Hand over the hard spots in your life to Jesus. He can turn your bitter clouds into sweet rain.

PLEASED

When people's lives please the LORD,
even their enemies are at peace with them.

PROVERBS 16:7 NLT

If children are trying to please their parents, they might make sure they eat all their vegetables and clean their room when told. At work, an employee will work harder when they want to please the boss or client. No matter the relationship, trying to please someone usually requires extra effort, going above and beyond.

With God, people have varying ideas on what pleases him. Living a morally upright life must please him. Or perhaps it's reading the whole Bible every year. Praying five times a day, fasting, confession, good deeds, sacrifice—these are all ways we attempt to please God. Though those things are not bad, they don't work. Nothing we can do works. What God requires us of us is faith in his Son. That's what pleases him. Faith. Those other things can bring us closer to God once we are saved, and they can help our spiritual development, but they can never be the way God is pleased with us.

God looks upon you, sees you in Christ, and is pleased. He is pleased with you! Be blessed in this.

HUNGER PANGS

LORD, save me by your power
from those whose reward is in this life.
They have plenty of food.
They have many sons and leave much money to their children.

PSALM 17:14 NCV

Did you make sure that you ate today? You were probably reminded at various times throughout the day that you felt hungry, and it's more than likely you answered that pang in your stomach. What if we had the same kind of triggers to remind us that we hadn't spent time with Jesus or weren't seeking after his wisdom?

What would those triggers be for you? It could be the times when you are confused, sad, or despairing. Often we will be reminded of God in those times. But could we also turn our joy into moments of desiring to be with him?

Set up reminders to draw near to God and follow through on them. It will only benefit you!

UNDER CONTROL

"I have brought you glory on earth by finishing the work you gave me to do."

John 17:4 NIV

As we walk in love, we will see fruit develop from what we do. We bring life and joy, truth and gentleness. We bring our gifts and ambitions. Sometimes this is met with delight and gratitude. Other times people don't understand our intentions. We may sow our gifts faithfully and never see good come of it. You may be feeding the poor and feeling heartbroken that there is not enough water. You may be clothing the naked and weeping that their bills won't be paid this month.

The point is this: You are being faithful. God is proud of you. And though the world around you may not understand what you are doing, and though you may not understand the world around you, Jesus has everything under control. He is making beautiful things in and with you. That is enough. Just walk with him in faith this morning.

Ask God to make you bold to trust him and to know that everything will be okay as you rest in him and walk through life.

TURNING BACK

The fire of the LORD fell and burned up the sacrifice, the wood, the stones and the soil, and also licked up the water in the trench. When all the people saw this, they fell prostrate and cried, "The LORD —he is God! The LORD —he is God!"

1 KINGS 18:38-39 NIV

There are times when God chooses to demonstrate his power. Throughout Scripture, we see a God who loves his people so much that he does what it takes to turn them back to him.

Don't become discouraged thinking that God is silent in this day and age. Our God is alive and powerful and willing to move in the hearts of those who have hearts that are open to him. Look around you and be willing to be a vessel through whom God can move.

If it seems like God is silent, keep asking. He will move when it is time, and you want to be ready when that happens.

CHILDLIKE

"Anyone who becomes as humble as this little child is the greatest in the Kingdom of Heaven."

MATTHEW 18:4 NLT

Children have so much to teach us about faith. A child will trust quickly, love boldly, and accept willingly. This is why Jesus commends us having faith like a child. It will require vulnerability and an open heart to trust the promises of the Scriptures.

We may be disappointed that our sacrificial love is not returned by those around us. And we may have to face having our trust broken even by other believers. But faith requires believing in the restoring power of Jesus. Faith means believing that things will work out for the best. Accepting the love of Jesus means you don't have to try to prove your worth to others.

Allow Jesus to take the baggage of doubts, insecurities, and fears away so you can live in the freedom of a secure future in Christ.

SEEING CLEARLY

The precepts of the Lord are right,
giving joy to the heart.
The commands of the Lord are radiant,
giving light to the eyes.

Psalm 19:8 NIV

You might have had to get glasses recently because the road signs have become fuzzy or out of focus. At times, our spiritual life needs this kind of attention. When life gets out of focus or things get dim, we need to turn a light on.

We need to turn to the Lord to bring things back into alignment again. This will make you feel like you are living in a world that appears brighter and clearer, just like putting on that new pair of prescription glasses. It doesn't have to be a major sin issue or crisis for our lives to get out of line. Business, monotonous tasks, and minor distractions can all skew our vision little by little.

Ask the Lord to search your heart and see if you need an adjustment today.

DESPERATE FOR YOU

And like newborn babies, long for the pure milk of the word, so that by it you may grow in respect to salvation.

1 Peter 2:2 NASB

To help us understand how intensely new Christians should seek to know all they can about God, Peter uses the image of a newborn baby. Nothing matters more to a baby than milk; it's a desperate, greedy, primal longing. It's quite a picture, and no doubt one we don't quite recall living up to. We may have felt passionate but not quite primal.

Minus the kicking and the crying, perhaps, can we not relate? When we first tasted God's goodness, did anything matter more? Was anything as sweet? Met with the incredible truth of his perfect love, did we think it possible we'd ever get enough? Just as a baby outgrows the one-track neediness of infancy, so we mature in our faith. Less desperate, we're content to take him in slowly, savoring each morsel of truth.

Are you hungry enough for the Lord? Do you still sense your need for him? If you've grown too comfortable, ask to be infused with a fresh, primal hunger for him.

HURLED INTO THE SEA

"You hurled me into the depths, into the very heart of the seas, and the currents swirled about me; all your waves and breakers swept over me. I said, 'I have been banished from your sight; yet I will look again toward your holy temple.'"

JONAH 2:3-4 NIV

It doesn't matter whether you feel like you are drowning because you have intentionally walked away from God or whether circumstances have simply overwhelmed you. Expressing how you feel about being distant from God or grace is important.

If you feel like this today, tell God. In the same way that you express your sorrow, be intentional about directing your words and heart toward God. Look toward his holy temple, not away from it. God is near and will answer your cries.

When you feel distant from God, choose to look toward him and trust him for answers.

ALIVE TOGETHER

God, being rich in mercy, because of His great love with which He loved us, even when we were dead in our wrongdoings, made us alive together with Christ (by grace you have been saved).

EPHESIANS 2:4-5 NASB

In areas of our lives where we see destruction and devastation, there is hope. We have been made alive with Christ in his resurrection. This means that whatever doesn't look fruitful is awaiting the redemption that God works within and for us. There is no situation too bleak that he cannot bring beauty and regeneration from it.

God is in the business of doing the impossible. What seems out of the question in our minds is an invitation to faith and trust in God's miracle-working power. We have been covered in grace that empowers us. He changes us from the inside out and brings beauty out of the ashes of despair. And he does it again and again! Let us hope in him, for he is surely not finished with us yet.

You cannot deplete God's love in your life. That reality is more wonderful than the highest of hopes. Ask the Holy Spirit to breathe on the barren parts of your heart and bring new life.

SMALL DELIGHTS

The believers met together in the Temple every day. They ate together in their homes, happy to share their food with joyful hearts.

ACTS 2:46 NCV

The office has become more than a place you go to get work done. You might not be there to socialize, but like it or not, it's a place where the same people gather almost every day and you will inevitably be sharing at least a few small things about your life here and there.

You probably also have closer friends from work that you might have lunch with, or at times your team will have a coffee break together. Sometimes this is where you get asked questions about your faith, your church, or your moral opinions. It can be uncomfortable, but try to see your workplace as an opportunity to share the light of Christ.

People know something is different about you when you respond most frequently with love and grace. Your joyful presence can stir up conversations about your faith. Be encouraged that others see God in you.

ELEVENTH HOUR

"Take what belongs to you and go. I choose to give to this last worker as I give to you."

MATTHEW 20:14 ESV

Today is the day! You might be very good at putting things off until the very last minute, just like those who receive their salvation when they are on their deathbed and finally see and accept the truth. The point of the parable of this Scripture, however, is that while everyone is accepted into the kingdom, it is more blessed to have lived a life journey that had the freedom, peace, and joy of walking with Christ.

Because you are aware that it is better to live this life with Christ, apply some urgency to sharing the hope of Jesus. Share your faith openly and bravely, knowing that it's better not to leave it to the last minute.

Share the message of hope with someone who needs to hear it before the eleventh hour.

UNSEEN MYSTERIES

"Have you believed because you have seen me? Blessed are those who have not seen and yet have believed."

John 20:29 ESV

The early years of childhood are filled with questions about things kids can't see with their eyes. "Is the Easter Bunny real?" "Do you think Santa put me on the nice list?" Without question, children desire to believe in something they can't see because of the joy it brings them. The mystery, magic, and excitement around certain events and holidays can be enough to stir their hearts into believing in those mysteries with all their might.

What a shame that we lose that faith as we get older. Can we be excited about the Creator of the universe—of all the mysteries we cannot see or don't yet understand? If we trust by faith and not by sight, we will be doubly blessed.

Even though you can't see God, you know he is real. You know he rules over the universe in all its granduer and down to the tiniest detail. That alone should cause you a certain amount of childlike wonder today.

SHOUT FOR JOY

May we shout for joy when we hear of your victory
and raise a victory banner in the name of our God.
May the LORD answer all your prayers.

PSALM 20:5 NLT

We often pray without expecting much of a response, so it is good to acknowledge those times when we see that God has answered our prayers. Some stories in Scripture help build our faith and so do the stories of our answered prayers. They are there to be shared.

You may have uttered many prayers and petitions; some might have been answered, others have not. Sometimes the answers you are hoping for are not the ones that come. You have to believe that God knows best. He sees the full picture and he will carry you through to victory—his way. Be encouraged today to continue to present your requests to God, knowing that he is listening.

Remember and share stories where you have witnessed God answering prayers. Let those accounts be an encouragement to those who hear them.

BLESSING UNTOLD

You make him most blessed forever;
you make him glad with the joy of your presence.

Psalm 21:6 ESV

The Psalmist declared that it was the Lord who had blessed him. First, David's worldly riches could be attributed to God placing him in his position as king, and second, the Lord's blessings far outweigh all of the earth's treasures. David was allotted both.

David was blessed forever because of his faith in the Lord, which leads to eternal life, but also because from his lineage the Messiah would be born—so his line continues forever. The Psalmist made it clear that David's joy was not from his position as king or all the glory he had accumulated on the earth. Rather, his joy came from being in the presence of the Lord.

Regardless of whether you are royalty or utterly destitute, your joy will come from being with God and spending time in his presence.

MORE THAN ANYTHING

My son, give me your heart,
and let your eyes observe my ways.

PROVERBS 23:26 CSB

What's the most valuable thing you have ever loaned out? Your car, perhaps? As you handed over the keys, you were telling this person you trusted them. You believed they would treat the car as their own. You also implied they were more important to you than any thing.

To give our hearts to someone requires even more trust. We place faith in their willingness to care for our feelings as their own, to want only good for us, and to value us as a treasure. We are taking a risk. Except, of course, when we give our hearts to the Lord. There is no risk in trusting God. The maker of our hearts will treat them better than his own. He considers us more important than not just any *thing* but *anything*, and he counts us as his treasure.

Trust God with your feelings, your future, and your hope. Give him your heart. Ask him to make you more loving to those you share your life with.

OPEN MY UNDERSTANDING

Then he opened their minds to understand the Scriptures.

Luke 24:45 ESV

Can you remember enjoying a book or film as a child, then revisiting it as an adult? How amazed were you to discover all you'd missed? It's like discovering the old, familiar painting in Grandma's attic is a masterpiece by a renowned artist. Our adult minds understand more of the humor, recognize layers of context, and interpret subtext in a way we couldn't as children.

When it comes to understanding Scripture, we are all as children. Different aspects of Christ's character are revealed as we grow and mature in our faith. God chooses when and how to enlighten us, so like that favorite childhood story or movie, every return to a Bible passage can hold fresh revelation.

Ask God to open your mind to the incredible, living truth of his Word. Thank him for making it eternally new.

FOCUSED ON HIM

You, Lord, give true peace to those who depend on you, because they trust you.

Isaiah 26:3 NCV

This world is full of great opportunities. So many, in fact, that we have even coined a term for people who don't like to miss out. *FOMO*. It's a real thing not just for the younger generation trying to decide which social event to attend, but for many of us. When we have FOMO, we keep saying yes to opportunities that may seem great, but they cause strain on the things God has already asked us to do. Here's the test: are you saying yes out of fear, or are you saying yes in peace?

God's peace can be a perfect indicator as to which category the yes falls into. Will your current calling suffer? Will you lay aside that creative endeavor God told you to pursue because this one makes money? Will you take on another volunteer role at your church even though God clearly told you to be in a season of rest? Don't live in FOMO. Live in peace.

Put your yes to the test. What is the underlying motive: fear or faith? God's peace can help you answer that question.

TAKING THE RISK

The LORD is my light and my salvation;
whom shall I fear?
The LORD is the stronghold of my life;
of whom shall I be afraid?

PSALM 27:1 ESV

Most great things in life take some risk. We probably can each say that we've taken some pretty dumb chances in life, but we have also taken some incredible ones. Some of our risks end in disaster, but others in sheer beauty.

One thing all risk has in common is that it teaches something. We never walk away unchanged. And while stepping out and taking the risk itself is scary, we discover our own bravery in it. Trusting God requires our faith, which is a risk. But taking a risk is necessary to follow God wholeheartedly. Of course, it's easier to sit on the sidelines. To slide under the radar. To live safe. But letting fear hold us back from taking a risk keeps us from the breathtaking possibilities of life.

Sometimes you just need to jump. Set aside your own understanding of situations and trust what God is saying to you. The kind of risk required for faith in him is the kind with the greatest reward.

HAVE DISCERNMENT

The wise see danger ahead and avoid it,
but fools keep going and get into trouble.

PROVERBS 27:12 NCV

What does it look like to be discerning? If we equate faith with blind belief, then we may dismiss the warnings of those who discern patterns and cycles as unbelief. But this is not what faith actually is. Our faith is rooted in the faithfulness of God. There is fruit to be found in this. There are patterns at work in this world that we can prepare for, knowing how to spot them.

We do not need to spiritually bypass real concerns, wishing away the negative sides of life. We can be prepared for inevitabilities and still rely fully on the Lord. We can look ahead and see how a relationship or job may fall apart because of the glaring red flags that are there now. We can avoid danger by dealing with the realities in the present. To be sure, there is grace and mercy to cover us. But there is also maturity in practicing discernment and in being selective about our choices.

Thank God for his wisdom that guides you. Lean into the discernment found in his Spirit, and in those who are naturally more able to see patterns and cycles.

A SINGLE GIFT

One thing I ask from the Lord, this only do I seek:
that I may dwell in the house of the Lord
all the days of my life,
to gaze on the beauty of the Lord
and to seek him in his temple.

Psalm 27:4 NIV

How old were you when you learned that the fewer gifts there were to unwrap at your birthday, the more valuable each package was? When we are presented with a single gift, we know to expect something truly special.

King David understood this perhaps better than anyone; forsaking all other requests, he went for the ultimate gift. *I just want to live with you, God. I want to see your beautiful face and visit you in your temple.* He knew that, were he to unwrap this precious package, every second of his life would be blessed.

Joy lives with God. Peace, contentment, and almost unbearable beauty—they all live with him too. Seek to live with him, so you can understand the value of that single, perfect gift.

BETTER DAYS

"If you look for me wholeheartedly, you will find me."

JEREMIAH 29:13 NLT

Remember playing hide-and-seek on a day you weren't really feeling it? You didn't find everyone because your heart wasn't really in the search. A halfhearted search for God—his will, his voice, his blessings—won't be any more productive. He absolutely wants to be found, but not until you're in the game, not until finding him is all you can think about.

In our faith journey, we don't want to simply go through the motions, stepping through doorways but not looking behind them, walking through hallways with our eyes straight ahead. We want to find God, so we go all in. We'll search everywhere, even the places we've already been. We throw our whole hearts into it because that's what I want from him.

Spend some honest time thinking about how dedicated you are to finding and being with God.

AUGUST

I did this so you would trust not in human wisdom but in the power of God.

1 Corinthians 2:5 NLT

SHIELD OF FAITH

In all circumstances take up the shield of faith, with which you can extinguish all the flaming darts of the evil one.

EPHESIANS 6:16 ESV

Just as a shield was a key accessory to a soldier in ancient Rome, so our faith is to us today. We never know when the enemy will try to attack us or break us down, so we must remain vigilant. The shield of faith is a big component to fighting and winning against the devil's onslaught. Without our faith, we are vulnerable, weak, and flawed humans; we are easy prey.

It is God who makes us strong, for he alone can overcome the enemy. In all circumstances, we must take up our shields and stand ready to use them by remaining in the Word, in prayer, and by staying attentive to what God is saying.

Ask God to give you strength and perseverance to withstand the darts of the enemy. Be ready to take up your shield of faith.

SHARED FEELINGS

Trust in Him at all times, you people;
Pour out your heart before Him;
God is a refuge for us.

Psalm 62:8 NASB

We like to spend time on our personal relationship with God, and yet there is more to our faith than just ourselves. We were created to be in community with one another and one really important benefit of a close community is that we can be encouraged, or encourage others, in times of distress.

Think of the last time you felt really anxious or discouraged and reflect on who you were able to share those feelings with. Together we can pour out our hearts to him. We are all on this journey, not just individually, but walking alongside each other. Take a moment today to encourage the people you are walking with through life.

Be intentional about developing close relationships with those who encourage you in your faith and with those you can also encourage.

EXCITING ADVENTURE

Since the world began, no ear has heard and no eye has seen a God like you, who works for those who wait for him!

Isaiah 64:4 NLT

Being a believer is not just another title to throw on the list of roles you hold. It should be a completely life-changing experience, affecting all areas of your reality. The Christian life is quite the adventure for the woman who submits herself to God's will. God gives each of us specific spiritual gifts; have you discovered yours? Looking into this can bring clarity and vitality to your life. Next, take God at his word. There are so many areas where we are asked to have big faith. If you want to see God move mountains, you must have faith.

Lastly, pray specifically, and keep track. When you write down your prayers and go back to look at them, you will find a pathway through all the ways God showed up in your life. It's thrilling to see God moving and answering our prayers.

If you feel like your walk with Christ is just another title, maybe it's time to do some self-examination.

IF ONLY

"My eyes will be open and My ears attentive to prayer made in this place. For now I have chosen and sanctified this house, that My name may be there forever; and My eyes and My heart will be there perpetually."

2 Chronicles 7:15-17 NKJV

God was so pleased that Israel had sought his presence because this is how he would be able to speak to them. When you have turned yourself toward the Lord, he is willing to see your circumstance and listen to your prayers.

It is not about you being a good person that gives you bargaining power; it is simply that you have turned to him and asked to be with him. His promise to you is that when you stay close to him, his eyes and heart will be with you forever.

Turn your face toward God now and ask him to fill you with assurance that he is forever with you, listening and responding like an attentive parent.

SAVING FAITH

The men at the table said among themselves, "Who is this man, that he goes around forgiving sins?" And Jesus said to the woman, "Your faith has saved you; go in peace."

LUKE 7:49-50 NLT

There was a lot of confusion in Jesus' day about who he really was. Many were expecting a different kind of Savior and often even Jesus' miracles weren't enough for people to believe that he was the true Messiah. This woman had faith to accept the Savior, to love him, and to seek forgiveness. Her faith and love for Christ saved her.

Jesus came to earth to show us a different way to live and love. When we acknowledge him as Lord, we will have peace, knowing our faith and salvation is in him.

Restore your faith in Jesus. Believe that he is the true Christ who can forgive all your sin and save you.

GOOD STORIES

I will tell everyone about your righteousness.
All day long I will proclaim your saving power,
though I am not skilled with words.

PSALM 71:15 NLT

Do you proclaim God's power all day long? It's good to remember that not everything expressed in the Psalms is literal. We use exaggerations as part of our language to emphasize the extremity of our feelings. Don't feel like you are less spiritual because you don't talk about Jesus every single moment of the day.

It is a good practice to tell others about how you have experienced God in your life. It can be a great witness to those who don't yet know him and an encouragement to those who do. Proclaim his grace at every opportunity even if you don't have the right words.

What amazing things do you have to tell about what God has done for this world and in your life? Take opportunities to share God's goodness with others.

EAGERLY WAITING

If we hope for what we do not see,
we eagerly wait for it with perseverance.

ROMANS 8:25 NKJV

There is blessing in the development of our faith. When we cannot see the physical representation of our hope, but we eagerly await its coming, gritty persistence keeps us expectant. May we be tenacious in faith, not letting go of the anticipation of our fulfilled longing. Whenever we grow a bit tired in believing, let us look to him who is steadfast in marvelous mercy. He will infuse us with strength.

What a glorious hope we have in him! The fulfillment of his promises is not dependent on our own reliability, but on his. We can be persistent in belief because it is based on his unchanging nature, not what we're waiting for. He is so much better than we can fully comprehend, so let's place our attention on his overwhelming goodness.

Look to Jesus today. He is your hope, your firm foundation, and the basis of your faith.

MOUNTAIN MOVER

What then shall we say to these things? If God is for us, who can be against us?

ROMANS 8:31 ESV

Mountains in nature are awe inspiring, beautiful, and majestic. Mountains in our lives are a different story. We often liken our troubles to mountains because of their looming nature, their size, and even the treacherous manner it takes to cross them. Faith allows us to see how much larger God is than our mountains. We stand at the base in disbelief. But faith zooms us out to a view that shows us that though there might be ranges of mountains in our future, God is more expansive than even the atmosphere that surrounds them.

Our focus has to be on how big God is. A lack of faith has an awful tendency to glue our feet to the ground, so we are unable to see anything but negativity. Those who walk in faith are people who admit they might not know how the mountain will be moved, but that God will supply no matter what.

God is the mountain mover. Pray for faith to arise, so you can see how big he is.

HOW RICH

You do well and excel in every respect—in unstoppable faith, in powerful preaching, in revelation knowledge, in your passionate devotion, and in sharing the love we have shown to you. So make sure that you also excel in grace-filled generosity.

2 Corinthians 8:7 TPT

Looking just at the first phrase of this verse, what do you imagine? Perhaps your thoughts turn to things, or maybe talents. Intellectual brilliance, impressive athleticism, and professional success come to mind. Yet, we see that Paul's standards are attainable for everyone.

We don't need talent to be faithful, money to gain knowledge, or skill to share love. We only need Christ. Through him we can excel in every way that matters. We can be infused with unstoppable faith. He will speak his truth through us and teach us, giving us passion to serve and share.

Continue to pray through this list of attributes, inviting the Lord to increase them in your heart and will.

PILGRIMAGE

Blessed are those whose strength is in you,
whose hearts are set on pilgrimage.

Psalm 84:5 NIV

We never really arrive at our spiritual destination of holiness, and that's the way it is meant to be. The beauty is found where the heart is inclined toward finding the presence of God. This is our journey of faith in Christ. It is a pilgrimage in every sense of the word.

It might be a long and difficult terrain to navigate, but there will be wonders to see along the way and some profound insights and thoughts as you progress. This pilgrimage is one that ends at the most beautiful of places, one that your heart cannot fully comprehend. Enjoy the journey that you are on today.

Your eternal destination is full of promise. Thank God for the journey that is leading you there. Appreciate the beauty of the walk today.

LOVE AND TRUTH

Your kingdom is built on what is right and fair.
Love and truth are in all you do.

PSALM 89:14 NCV

What is your faith worth? How far are you willing to go to express the love of God to a dying world? Will you give of yourself when it isn't convenient? Will you love someone who seems unlovable or give to someone who can never repay you?

The cost may seem great and the work insignificant, but God sees your heart and what you have done, and he counts it as work done directly for him.

Show your faith in action toward those in need. Ask the Holy Spirit to guide you to the needs of others, and respond quickly when he does.

GOD FIRST

Am I now seeking the approval of man, or of God? Or am I trying to please man? If I were still trying to please man, I would not be a servant of Christ.

GALATIANS 1:10 ESV

For many of us, we love the approval we get from pleasing others. But human praise is fickle. We all have varying opinions and preferences, and the requests of this world ebb and flow like waves in the ocean. Instead, let us seek to please God above all others.

The Word of God says that God is easy to please. This is good news for those of us who believe. We don't need to strive to attain his favor; we already have it in Christ. Jesus says in Matthew 11:29, "Simply join your life with mine. Learn my ways and you'll discover that I'm gentle, humble, easy to please" (tpt). It is much better to follow the ways of Jesus, joining our lives with his, and seeking to please him. He is so patient with us, even in our failures and wandering.

Remember that God's approval is more important than the accolades of others. Thank him for his patience with you.

WAYS TO REMEMBER

Our Lord Jesus Christ has shown me that I must soon leave this earthly life, so I will work hard to make sure you always remember these things after I am gone.

2 Peter 1:14-15 NLT

It is as important to remind others of Christ's love as it is to be reminded of it yourself. Each generation of Christians that have gone before us have left their Mark on the world because they shared Jesus through their actions and deeds. In the same way, you are able to pass on Christ's love through what you say and do. This isn't to be experienced as a burden but as a joy.

The impact of your faith can influence many generations to come. Be encouraged that God can work through you so others will know of his love.

Keep motivated to pass on the blessing of faith that you have been graciously given.

FOOLS FOR HIM

It is written: "I will destroy the wisdom of the wise, and bring to nothing the understanding of the prudent."

1 CORINTHIANS 1:19 NKJV

At the end of the day, you may feel like you have not made a significant impact on anything or anyone. Be encouraged that today you were an example of the living God and that your life shares good news whether you feel like you have or not.

Each day that you continue to have faith in Jesus Christ, you are carrying the good news. Sometimes you just need to look for opportunities to share it. You don't have to say all the right words. You can just speak from your heart. God's wisdom is not like the world's. When you speak his words, you cut through lies and cause hope to stir in people's hearts.

You carry God with you each day. Look for situations where you can share his good news. He will give you the right words at the right time.

ETERNAL LEGACY

All flesh is like grass and all its glory like the flower of grass. The grass withers, and the flower falls, but the word of the Lord remains forever.

1 Peter 1:24-25 ESV

We are made in the image of God, but we bear flesh while we are on this temporary earth. Our flesh will pass away, but our souls are eternal. Young and old, humans die at various times. But our glory is like the flower. Our earthly doings may leave a legacy for a few hundred years, but they are not eternal. We can write great books, produce awesome films, compose amazing music, construct complex buildings, and run large companies, but those aren't eternal legacies.

The Word of the Lord remains forever and finds its source in God. God is forever. Things that bring him glory and honor remain forever. Loving your neighbor well has eternal value, as does humbly serving your family, being faithful to your spouse, fighting for justice, and defending the fatherless.

When you analyze your life, what kind of legacy do you think you are leaving? Choose the legacy of God today.

READY HELP

God, hurry to help me, run to my rescue!
For you're my Savior and my only hope!

Psalm 38:22 TPT

Have you ever read through Psalms and thought, *Wow! David was in a lot of trouble in his life.* The truth is that he had a wealth of human experiences. We tend to put heroes of faith on a pedestal, forgetting to account for the weakness of their humanity. David was far from perfect, but he was rescued by God time and time again.

Is this because he earned it? No. It is because he kept turning to the Lord, crying out to him as often as he was in need. He loved the Lord and built his life upon him. He messed up, repented, and gave thanks to the Lord—over and over again. He lived with relationship with God as his ultimate goal. He never stopped going to him, in times of celebration and in times of desperation.

Take David's lead and go straight to God. He is your help and he will not fail you when you cry out to him.

GREAT FAITH

The LORD was with Joseph and showed him steadfast love and gave him favor in the sight of the keeper of the prison. The keeper of the prison paid no attention to anything that was in Joseph's charge, because the LORD was with him. And whatever he did, the LORD made it succeed.

GENESIS 39:21, 23 ESV

When looking for models of faith and perseverance, we needn't look further than Joseph, son of Jacob, from the Old Testament. Stripped, thrown into a well, and sold into slavery by his own brothers, then jailed for a crime he didn't commit, Joseph is a timeless example of how God's blessings can supersede our circumstances.

Because of his great faith, Joseph didn't just survive slavery and imprisonment, he thrived; so much so, he became the second-highest official in Egypt. Joseph loved God so much that he felt his presence everywhere he went. This allowed him to experience joy and success in the worst of circumstances and least likely of places.

Remember that though many things are out of your control, you always have at least one choice: to love, trust and obey God.

FIRMLY

Stay true to the Lord. I love you and long to see you, dear friends, for you are my joy and the crown I receive for my work.

PHILIPPIANS 4:1 NLT

The mother faced down her opposer, determined to win the battle. She had said no when he voiced his viewpoint on the subject. She knew her reasons were justified, but her rival wouldn't budge. He had dug in his heels and refused to see things her way. Out of intense love for her toddler and for her own sanity, she stood her ground. She scooped him up, carrying the boy off for the nap he refused but definitely needed.

Did you know you are the apple of God's eye? His love for us is extravagant, and as our loving Father, he always works for good on our behalf. He sees our today and our tomorrow, and he alone can understand what we need before we even ask. He knows what he has called us to do for his kingdom, and he equips us to achieve it. He leads us to become more like his Son, transforming us into his likeness. He tells us to trust his ways and stand securely in our faith. When trials come, he will fight our battles for us as he leads us into victory for his glory.

Ask for strength where you are wavering or insecure in your faith.

HOLD ONTO TRUTH

Those false teachers are so eager to win your favor, but their intentions are not good. They are trying to shut you off from me so that you will pay attention only to them.

GALATIANS 4:17 NLT

It is important to be vigilant and sure of the Christian faith. There are so many faith alternatives out there, and while we all express the Christian faith differently, there are some core beliefs that we need to stand firm on.

When you hear others speak about Christianity in a way that is different to what you believe, make sure to question their motives. If they seem like they have selfish intentions, go back to the simple truth of the message you read in the Bible; this is your true assurance of faith in Christ.

Ask God for wisdom and discernment to know what is truth and what is merely human pride.

THE UNSEEN

We don't focus our attention on what is seen but on what is unseen. For what is seen is temporary, but the unseen realm is eternal.

2 Corinthians 4:18 TPT

What we focus our attention on matters. God's kingdom is full of the treasures found in his unfailing love. When we spend our time caught up in the changing circumstances of our lives without grounding ourselves in the reality of eternity, it can be overwhelming.

When we shift our awareness to God's character, we are looking with eyes that see the promise of his kingdom come because he is faithful to do all he said he would. Let us fix our eyes on God, the author and perfecter of our faith. He never wavers in kindness, and his compassion never ends. They are as eternal as God himself. When we look for evidence of his goodness, we will surely find it.

Fix your eyes on God and eternity rather than on momentary troubles. Ask for his perspective, so you can see as he does.

TRUE WORSHIPPERS

"A time is coming and has now come when the true worshipers will worship the Father in the Spirit and in truth, for they are the kind of worshipers the Father seeks. God is spirit, and his worshipers must worship in the Spirit and in truth."

JOHN 4:23-24 NIV

The Samaritan woman had lived an immoral lifestyle. She was more than simply physically thirsty; she was spiritually thirsty too. She had transitioned from relationship to relationship until becoming an outcast in society. When confronted by Jesus at the well, she asked him where true worshippers ought to worship—fixated on the location. Jesus' response to her in this verse was profound.

It did not matter where geographically she worshipped, so long as it was in spirit and in truth. God saw into her spirit, saw the sin, and desired her anyway. He wanted her to come before him in truth and find forgiveness and love. Furthermore, Jesus offered to vanquish her dryness with his love. She would never need to grow spiritually thirsty again because of his fully satisfying relationship.

Jesus' everlasting love fills every crevice of your heart. No other relationship will satisfy your longing the way he does because your heart was created to love him.

DISCOURAGEMENT

They bribed officials to work against them and frustrate their plans during the entire reign of Cyrus king of Persia and down to the reign of Darius king of Persia.

EZRA 4:5 NIV

People can go over and above to try and stop something that they don't believe in. You might not have felt any persecution for your faith, but it is always good to be praying for the advancement of the kingdom.

We don't want to see God's restoration plan be stalled on account of the world's neglect of the truth. Rather than allowing the enemy to get a foothold, defend the gospel and make sure that God's Word, and his church, prevails. He is more powerful and knowing than anything or anyone on earth. He already knows the plans in place to stop his kingdom from advancing. He will not be stopped.

Don't be discouraged. Ask for discernment to know when and how to pray for a breakthrough.

LOOK NO FURTHER

Since we have been justified by faith, we have peace with God through our Lord Jesus Christ.

Romans 5:1 ESV

Let us be reminded, right here and now, that peace with God is not unattainable. It is ours through faith in Jesus. Faith is not simply a set of beliefs; it spills over into how we live our lives. We can rest assured that peace with God is ours, letting everything else flow from that place. We do not strive to be made righteous, for we are covered in the mercy-love of God that has made us right with him.

As we journey through this life in relationship with God, submitting our hearts to him regularly, he teaches and guides us in the ways of his laid-down love. The love offering of our lives is a natural response to the one who laid down his own for us. He has everything we need—and even more than that, all that we long for.

You stand covered in the mercy of God's love because he has made you clean. There is nothing you could ever add or take away from Jesus' finished work on the cross.

CONSTRUCTION WORKERS

Encourage one another and build one another up, just as you also are doing.

1 Thessalonians 5:11 NASB

Do you like to build things? Most kids love tiny, colorful building blocks, and they create all sorts of wonderful worlds out of them. Some of us grew up to make building our profession, constructing houses, roads, and skyscrapers. In the Christian faith, God asks all of us to be builders. When we participate in the growth of another believer, we build.

You are called a temple of God when you become a believer. You are a temple alone, but also a part of the whole body of Christ, a sanctuary being built with Christ as the cornerstone. When we encourage each other in the faith, we are building a better house. The temple is where the Holy Spirit dwells. We can use our words and actions to build a better house for the Holy Spirit—one of unity and love. It's amazing how God works through his people.

Join God in building today. Encourage other believers in their faith.

HE IS WILLING

He put out His hand and touched him, saying, "I am willing; be cleansed." Immediately the leprosy left him.

LUKE 5:13 NKJV

We have to ask Jesus for help, but we also have to wait for him to respond. With great faith comes a great wait. Sometimes it is quick, other times it is not. Be assured, as the Scripture says that Jesus is always willing to work in your life.

It is interesting that the man is asking to become clean rather than healthy, but Jesus makes him whole in every respect—body, mind, and heart. Jesus is always willing to make us whole. We just need wisdom to know when we are seeing healing a different way than he is.

Ask for great faith to believe in the total healing of God. He is willing to heal you.

CONTINUOUS FAITH

These things I have written to you who believe in the name of the Son of God, that you may know that you have eternal life, and that you may continue to believe in the name of the Son of God.

1 John 5:13 NKJV

Some of us have been raised believing that faith in Jesus is a one-time deal. You hear the gospel, say the sinner's prayer, and that's it! You've gained your ticket to heaven, and you can go on living however you please. That is just a partial truth. Upon hearing the gospel and feeling the conviction of the Holy Spirit for sin, it is as simple as praying to Jesus to save you. But then, God is not done giving you grace with that one-time transaction. You must continue to believe.

It doesn't mean that you can slip up and lose your salvation if you have a rough day, but God wants you to continue to apply his grace to your life daily. Coming to faith in Jesus should change your life, and then continue to change it until you die. Faith is an ongoing process of changing your worldview to be eternally minded.

Continue to believe in Jesus and apply grace to your every situation.

COME HOME

God has made all things new, and reconciled us to himself, and given us the ministry of reconciling others to God.

2 Corinthians 5:18 TPT

God wanted you back. You may not have even realized you were separated, but God did, and he moved heaven and earth to get you back. How loved you are; how loved we all are! Just think of what he did for us, sacrificing his perfect Son so we could come home, fully reconciled, to him.

It is part of our mission to bring others back to him as well. He's not asking us all to become missionaries, or traveling evangelists, or to go door-to-door. He will ask this of some, but for most of us, he is simply asking us to live these brand-new lives in the open. Our light will be a magnet, our joy contagious. Drawn to us, they'll find him—and come home.

Don't keep the amazing joy of life with God hidden. Through his Spirit, do your part to reconcile others to God.

FAITH IN LOVE

The important thing is faith—the kind of faith that works through love.

GALATIANS 5:6 NCV

Many around you need a dose of faith: of believing in something higher than themselves. They need someone to tell them they are treasured, and they are seen. Hopelessness is a reality in the world today and it comes in varying forms.

God says love is the framework for faith. You can spread love in a beautiful way: a love that paves the way for faith, a love that speaks volumes to the Jesus you serve, a love that is inconceivable to the one draped in hopelessness. As you seek God's love in a greater way, he will give you more to spread. Everyone has struggles.

As you interact with people each day, remember to show faith in love.

FAITH OR SIGHT

We are always confident and know that as long as we are at home in the body we are away from the Lord. For we live by faith, not by sight.

2 Corinthians 5:6-7 NIV

Sometimes we demand a lot of God. "God, I'd like this house," "That is my dream Job," "I'm so ready to get married," and we wait in expectation. We wait for him to do the impossible. We wait for him to give us the desires of our hearts. Because if he does, then he is most definitely all-powerful. If he does, he heard our cry and answered. If he does, he loves us. This is living by sight.

In 2 Corinthians, it says we live by faith, not sight. We often doubt God. Living by faith is giving up any control we thought we had, and sitting in the passenger seat in eager anticipation of where God is taking us. His desires for us are great. He wants only the best, and he asks for our faith in return.

Let go of unfulfilled desires and start living by faith.

EAGER FOR MORE

Now is the time for us to progress beyond the basic message of Christ and advance into perfection. The foundation has already been laid for us to build upon: turning away from our dead works to embrace faith in God.

HEBREWS 6:1 TPT

God has an unlimited capacity to teach and enlighten us. Even a verse you've read a dozen times can take on a new meaning when you listen closely to his voice. Think of your faith as a fishing boat. The further you row from shore, the bigger the fish get. Grab the oars and row.

Don't be satisfied with knowing about God, actually get to know him. Take delight in your salvation and savor his complexity. Turn your back on sin and toward a life of great meaning. Get ready to row far away from the shore.

Invite God to take you into the deep waters where you have to solely trust in his goodness and faithfulness.

COMPELLED

Those who want to make a good impression outwardly are trying to compel you to be circumcised. The only reason they do this is to avoid being persecuted for the cross of Christ.

GALATIANS 6:12 NIV

Have you ever been cornered by a smooth, fast-talking salesperson? The encounter begins with simple conversation, but soon you are being told that your life has been drab and empty without the item he is selling. It doesn't matter if you can't afford it; you can't live without it.

In the early church, there were some who still held fast to Jewish law and believed that those who were not circumcised, should be. They were insistent that this was a necessity, but in truth, they were just trying to avoid opposition from the Jewish opponents of Christianity. In other words, they were looking out for themselves and placed this physical act above the sacrifice of Christ. The apostle Paul opposed this and encouraged the Galatians that the cross was enough. Christ is all sufficient. He defeated the grave and brought salvation. Nothing other than faith in Jesus is needed.

Don't try to do things that will make your position in Christ more secure. Trust in him alone.

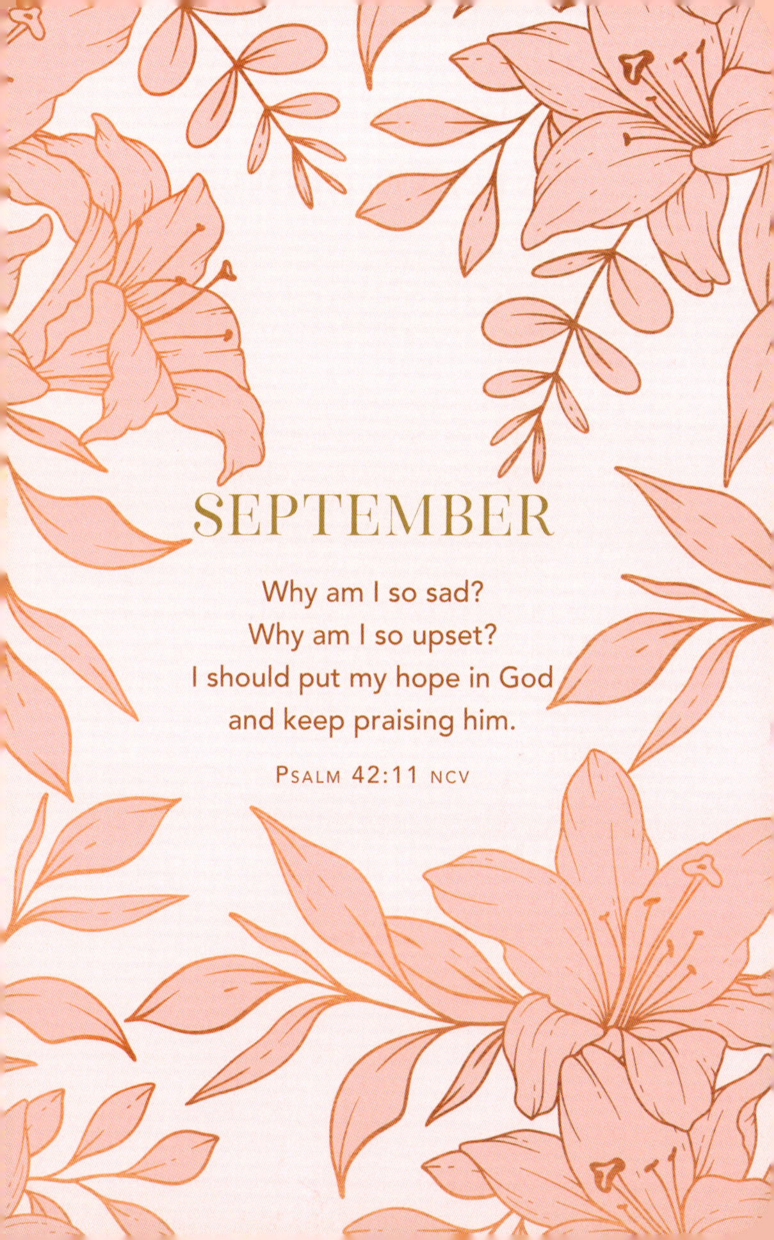
SEPTEMBER
Why am I so sad?
Why am I so upset?
I should put my hope in God
and keep praising him.
PSALM 42:11 NCV

WITHOUT LIMIT

Your faithfulness flows from one generation to the next;
all that you have created sits firmly in place to testify of you.

Psalm 119:90 TPT

What's the oldest thing you own? How long have you had it, and what does it mean to you? Whether a decades-old diamond ring, a twenty-year-old car, or a tattered baby blanket hanging together by threads, you probably know it won't last forever. How about your longest relationship? How many years have you been connected through good and bad?

One way you decide where to place your faith is longevity. History matters. You can carry on the faithfulness of the generations as you go about your day. Take Jesus with you in your heart and actions. Life with him is the most real thing you will ever know.

When you begin to doubt God, remind yourself that his love has been around since the beginning of time.

RUN FREE

Since we are surrounded by so great a cloud of witnesses, let us also lay aside every weight, and sin which clings so closely, and let us run with endurance the race that is set before us.

HEBREWS 12:1 ESV

In 2020, the world faced a pandemic that shut down many large gatherings including sports events. When sporting events reopened at first, they had to do most of their seasons without fans. Many athletes commented on how difficult it was. It was hard to perform their best without the cheering and support of their fans.

Here, the writer of Hebrews is describing our Christian faith like a marathon. In this event, we are not like the athletes of 2020 who had to play without the encouragement of their fans. Those who have gone before us in the faith, from the beginning until now, are all telling their stories as a sort of cheering section for us. They wave banners that say, "Keep your eyes on Christ!" "Run with perseverance!" "It's worth it!" You can find their testimonies in Scripture, in books, and from the mouths of those around you. Hear their encouraging shouts, and keep running.

Draw encouragement from your favorite testimony today.

PIONEER AND PROTECTOR

Let us run with endurance the race that lies before us, keeping our eyes on Jesus, the pioneer and perfecter of our faith. For the joy that lay before him, he endured the cross, despising the shame, and sat down at the right hand of the throne of God.

HEBREWS 12:1-2 CSB

After introducing so many heroes of the faith in Hebrews 11, the writer encourages Christians to draw confidence from their testimonies and similarly throw off anything which would hinder them from running the spiritual race that has been set before them.

The way we can endure all hardship and persevere is by keeping our eyes locked on Jesus. There are limitless distractions in this life, but Christ stands as an unadulterated paradox to them all. His faith was focused and flawless. Now he has given us that same faith and an unmatched example to follow.

Amidst the anguish of Jesus' sacrifice, he experience joy because of his great love for you. Ask him to strengthen you to run the race he has given you to run.

ABOVE ALL ELSE

"For where your treasure is, there your heart will be also."

LUKE 12:34 NASB

Treasure. It's an intriguing word, conjuring images of sunken chests filled with jewels, or ancient tombs overflowing with gold. As a noun, a treasure is something or someone of great value; as a verb, it means to guard carefully and to cherish. What do you value and protect? According to the Word, our answer will give us insight into the condition of our heart.

Outside of people and things, we may treasure intangibles, such as our reputations, talents and time. If we protect our reputation instead of promoting his, we miss opportunities to shine his light. When we care more for our talents than the one who bestowed them on us, we fail to use them for his glory. If we value our time too dearly, we will lose out on time with him. Our treasure should be with him, so our heart will be also.

Make Jesus the treasure of your heart today. Take back the pieces you have given or left elsewhere and let him have your time, talent, and reputation. Treasure the opportunity to glorify him.

THE BEAUTIFUL PRIZE

Above all else, let love be the beautiful prize for which you run.

1 Corinthians 13:13 TPT

What do you long for the most in this life? Is it beauty, success in your career, to get married, to have children? Do you want to do something of significance like write a book or come up with a new invention? These are all valid. And we all have gifts to use that can help us achieve them. They are God-given gifts, so don't ignore them!

When it comes to the kingdom of heaven, there is really nothing that goes beyond your faith, your hope for restoration, and love. This Scripture highlights that love surpasses them all. It was the love of God that created us, the love of Jesus that saved us, and the love of the Holy Spirit that keeps reminding us that we are loved. Walk in this love and let everything else fall in step with this beautiful prize.

Is love the prize you are striving for? Show someone God's love today.

LASTING VIRTUES

Three things will last forever—faith, hope, and love—
and the greatest of these is love.

1 CORINTHIANS 13:13 NLT

When everything else fades away in life, there are three things that remain unchanged: confident trust based on God's good character and faithfulness, hopeful expectation of the fulfillment of God's promises, and love that conquers all fears.

God's love is greater than any force known in the heavens or on the earth. It is strong enough to defeat death, powerful enough to make the sick well, and faithful enough to cover every living thing that has ever existed. Where we have been limited in love, may God's mercy meet us in new ways that blow open every box that we put it in. His compassion is wider reaching than we could ever comprehend.

Look for evidence of God's limitless love today and know that he is much better than you could ever give him credit for.

NEVER GIVE UP

Love never gives up, never loses faith, is always hopeful, and endures through every circumstance.

1 Corinthians 13:7 NLT

You might not feel like you are the best witness of Christ's love even though you know this is one of our greatest commandments. Don't worry; you are not alone. It is hard to know where to begin in sharing your faith to others. You might hope that someone will ask you about it one day and be open to hearing what you have to say. You might decide to be intentional about saying something but then lose courage halfway through the day.

Keep praying and developing your relationship with Jesus so you feel blessed, rather than ashamed, of your faith. Recognize that it is Jesus who helps you to never give up, to be hopeful, and to endure through every circumstance. Ask Jesus to help you come up with a way to express your faith.

Write out this encouraging Scripture and leave it somewhere you can see it often. Remind yourself of God's faithfulness.

LOTS OF ROOM

"There are many rooms in my Father's house; I would not tell you this if it were not true. I am going there to prepare a place for you."

JOHN 14:2 NCV

When our faith looks limited and is not expanding, it is time to reconsider what we are believing about God. Jesus made it clear that the love of God is not exclusive; it is bigger than anyone could ever imagine. It is larger than the universe, more powerful than any pressure in this world. It is indescribable in its great strength and capacity.

What would it look like to expand our faith in Jesus' love today? There are endless possibilities of goodness in his mercy. May we live with generous compassion, knowing that no matter where someone is in this life, the love of Jesus is powerful to save and transform even the hardest heart. May we reflect how generous Jesus is in the way that we live our lives.

Where you have grown cynical, let the mercy and kindness of God soften you with the unbridled hope of his powerful affection.

STEP OF FAITH

He said, "Come." And when Peter had come down out of the boat, he walked on the water to go to Jesus.

MATTHEW 14:29 NKJV

Jesus called us to come. He did not say it would be easy. The road is riddled with difficulties. He may call someone to give their money to the poor, someone else to move to the farthest corner of the world, or another to be faithful in their daily grind at home. He may lead us to serve a family or to find contentment with him in our singleness.

Are you lacking a purpose, feeling overwhelmed by your workload, or simply missing connection with God? Take a step of faith. Climb out of the boat and trust him. Even if you start to sink, and we all will from time to time, he is right beside you, ready to catch you. On whatever road he leads you, take his hand and trust him.

The only path to life is in Jesus. No matter what he has called you to, take his hand and trust him. He will never let you go.

BEAR THE WEAK

We who are strong ought to bear with the failings of the weak and not to please ourselves.

ROMANS 15:1 NIV

The context of the direction Paul is giving to believers who are stronger in their faith is when sin is not specifically the issue, but rather topics which are vague or culturally influenced. Earlier, Paul addressed issues such as eating meat, drinking alcohol, or celebrating questionable holidays. If someone weaker in the faith feels compelled to act a certain way, it is better for them to abstain rather than go against their conscience.

It is also better for those who are more mature in their faith to support those who are weaker in their journey of understanding the Lord rather than obnoxiously revel in their freedom in front of them. Although the Bible may not ask us to abstain from certain things, our abstinence may be necessary since the faith of our brothers and sisters is more important than our own pleasure.

Rather than judge or challenge others who are wrestling through where they stand, have the patience and insight to support and encourage them. Lay down your rights for their sake.

RESPOND IN LOVE

"If the world hates you, know that it has hated me before it hated you. If you were of the world, the world would love you as its own; but because you are not of the world, but I chose you out of the world, therefore the world hates you."

JOHN 15:18-19 ESV

The debate team was entering the competition arena. They were ready to meet their rivals and present their argument confidently. Their class had carefully studied tactics to attack sharply differing views from a stance of emotional indifference. However, as the topic grew heated, each student took words spoken about their subject to heart, and it became obvious that the intent to remain unmoved had been unsuccessful. Bad feelings were evident in the attitudes of the participants.

Jesus warned us that the world would not understand our belief or commitment to him. Some would see us as lunatics or as snobs, assuming we think ourselves higher than others. Opposers ridicule and try to silence believers. In some areas of the world, Christians are persecuted, tortured by evil organizations who insist they recant their faith or endure more torment. This is heartbreaking but not surprising, for Jesus said the world would hate us. When they do, we must respond in love.

As tensions in the world heighten, be prepared to stand firm for your faith.

ABIDE

"Abide in Me, and I in you. As the branch cannot bear fruit itself, unless it abides in the vine, neither can you, unless you abide in Me."

JOHN 15:4 NKJV

Abide is possibly one of the most important words in the Bible. It is essential to the believer's life to learn how to abide in Christ. To abide means to dwell. Think of your home. What's the difference between a house and a home? A house is just a structure. You feel comfortable and safe in a home. It's the place you can most be yourself and let your guard down.

God did not send his Son to create distance between him and humanity. He sent his Son to dwell with us, be close to us, and draw us closer to himself. God wants you to be at your most vulnerable and open in his presence. We are trained well in the art of superficial relationships. It is now time, through study of the Word and prayer, to learn how to have a deep relationship with Jesus. He is trustworthy and kind. Abiding in Christ will lead to obedience to his Word, and it will also lead to fruit for his glory. Jesus is calling you to come home today, to dwell with him and learn from him.

Sit with Jesus today and learn. Answer his call to abide.

SPIRITUAL ACHIEVEMENT

Whatever things were written before were written for our learning, that we through the patience and comfort of the Scriptures might have hope.

ROMANS 15:4 NKJV

You can get a new manicure every week. You can get in a good workout and drink all green juices and take vitamins. Go to college, get a masters, get a PHD. You can snag that promotion and make those zeros line up in your bank account. You can outfit your kids in the cutest clothes, stick cute notes in their healthy lunches, and show up for every PTA event. You can hustle and work and achieve like mad, but if you aren't rooted in the Word of God, what are you doing?

Everything that the world hands to us as hope will crumble into ash and blow away. All that remains is his Word, his promises, himself. Yesterday, today, and forever. That is the greatest pursuit and achievement you can gain.

Dig deep into God's Word today. Remove roadblocks that keep you from it and let it become your lifeline.

A YES FAITH

Abram believed the Lord. And the Lord accepted Abram's faith, and that faith made him right with God

GENESIS 15:6 NCV

Have you ever stepped out and said yes to something crazy for God? You followed him into the middle of the ocean and trusted him to keep you afloat. Stepping out in faith isn't easy. In fact, it's messy. It's a lot of wondering what you're doing, and why you're doing it. It's a lot of closing your eyes and begging God to remind you of all the things he placed on your heart when he originally gave you the vision. When you stand in the truth that you have obeyed, it doesn't really matter how everything looks or feels. What matters is that you were obedient. You believed what God was telling you.

Stepping out in faith is about boldly facing your harshest critics and telling them you're not sure if everything will work out. It's being at peace in total chaos. It's putting yourself out there and wondering if you'll live up to expectation. It's wondering if you have anything to offer after all.

There is peace in obedience. If God is asking you to do something that terrifies you, step out in faith. Obey him. Believe him. It will be worth it.

FAITHFUL AND STRONG

Be on your guard; stand firm in the faith;
be courageous; be strong.

1 Corinthians 16:13 NIV

In his final words to the church in Corinth, Paul gives this beautiful admonishment to help them hold onto the freedom they had found in Christ. A few thousand years later, this simple advice remains helpful. Be on your guard. Pay attention to the ways the enemy is trying to disrupt your peace and steal your joy. Stand firm in the faith. Temptation to compromise is a sure sign we are being messed with. Would you do or say it if Jesus was sitting right beside you? Well he is, so decide accordingly.

Be courageous. Over and over, the Lord tells us not to be afraid. Remember, there is no fear in love. If you are feeling afraid, reject fear and hold onto Christ—onto love. Be strong. What must you do to gain strength? Work, train, or try? Do it. Be strong.

Thank God for making the really important lessons so easy to find and follow. Watch, be faithful, be brave, and be strong—in him.

LOSING TO GAIN

"If you try to hang on to your life, you will lose it. But if you give up your life for my sake, you will save it."

MATTHEW 16:25 NLT

The key to growing in our faith is simple. There must be less of us in order to have more of God. To allow more of his presence into our lives, we must give up more of ourselves. We need to place our lives before him as an offering and give him our all.

The world would say that giving up ourselves is a loss. We've been taught for years that we must put ourselves first. Our fellow man would say that we need to make ourselves a priority. But oh, are they missing out! When we give ourselves over completely to God, we get to share in his glory and in his great joy. Setting aside our earthly pleasures for heavenly treasures means we gain a lot more than what this world could ever offer us.

Empty yourself of the desires of your flesh and allow God to fill you with his presence. You won't feel a lack. In fact, it will overflow in your life, spilling out everywhere for others to see!

THE REST WILL FOLLOW

Believe on the Lord Jesus Christ, and you will be saved, you and your household.

ACTS 16:31 NKJV

It is amazing and delightful to consider how highly God values faith. Abraham believed in the Lord, and was declared righteous as a result. When you consider God's faithfulness and choose to believe what he tells you, he will move mountains for you. When you trust him to forgive you and lead you for the rest of your life, your family will choose him as well.

How good our heavenly Father is, that he would not only save you, but also your household! Sitting before you each day are students who have families. As you pray for each of your unsaved family members, remember your students in prayer. God will hear your prayers and will bless their families.

Believe in the power of Jesus today. He is your salvation and your strength.

CALL UPON HIM

Oh, give thanks to the LORD! Call upon His name;
Make known His deeds among the peoples!

1 CHRONICLES 16:8 NKJV

In this moment, you have an opportunity. Every moment, every breath, is a chance to call upon the Lord. Raise your awareness and turn your attention to him. With a whispered prayer or a shout for help, call upon the Lord your God. He is always near. He is always full of strength and power to help you.

Has the Lord helped you? Tell someone. Has he turned ashes into beauty in your life? Share your story with someone who needs a boost of hope. Has he provided in unexpected ways? Thank him and disclose it to a friend. He is always at work, even when you cannot perceive it. When you recognize his incredible mercy, be encouraged and share it, so that faith may be increased and courage bolstered.

Call upon the name of the Lord today. Turn to him in your troubles and in your gratitude. He is faithful.

MUSTARD SEED

"You don't have enough faith," Jesus told them. "I tell you the truth, if you had faith even as small as a mustard seed, you could say to this mountain, 'Move from here to there,' and it would move. Nothing would be impossible."

MATTHEW 17:20 NLT

Faith is what binds us to God's will. It gives us a sense of what God desires and helps us believe that he can make it happen. It is not so much us getting God to do what we want to happen, but rather God getting us to ask for what he desires. With faith, we can ask for the right things and believe that God is powerful enough to make them happen.

Jesus said that if we have faith like a grain of mustard seed, mountains will move. Many people misinterpret this phrase. They believe that they can only move mountains if they have incredible amounts of faith. But the measure of our accomplishments is a measure of God's strength, working through us while we pray to be as faithful as we can, even if our faith feels as small as a mustard seed.

Anything is possible with God. Don't let your faith be limited by fear or doubt.

WHAT WE KNOW

In the morning, LORD, you hear my voice;
in the morning I lay my requests before you
and wait expectantly.

PSALM 3:5 NIV

Have you ever prayed for a greater measure of faith? If you haven't, it probably never occurred to you. Isn't faith believing? I believe in God, therefore I have faith, right? Why would I need more? Consider a rickety bridge across a great canyon. Using our eyes, we can see the bridge goes from one end of the canyon to the other, and that it just delivered a group of people safely to the other side. We saw, and so we believe. Old wood, old rope, and a high wind, however, can limit our faith in the bridge to do the same for us.

Despite everything we know about our loving, powerful, and gracious God, we still face things that run up to the limits of our faith. How blessed we are that we can always ask for more.

Each time you hesitate to ask for something you fear God might not choose to give, before he gives it, ask him to forgive you and increase your faith.

INCREASE OUR FAITH

The apostles said to the Lord, "Increase our faith."

LUKE 17:5 NLT

When we read that the people who were closest to Jesus asked him to increase their faith, it should help us to see that it's okay to ask for help. The apostles witnessed Jesus doing miracles with their own eyes, and they still weren't totally convinced. We do not have to be afraid of our doubts. We can confront them, ask God to help us see clearly, and put our faith in him.

Being honest about our lack of faith is not a sin but trying to hide it or ignore it can lead to worse consequences. When we stuff down our doubts, they don't go away. They pile up under the surface until we end up with more questions than answers, and our faith sits on a very unstable foundation. God desires us to ask him the hard questions, so that he can either answer them and give us insight, or not, but still increase our faith.

Ask God to increase your faith. Confess your doubt and commit to being better about putting your trust in him.

LIVING WATER

"He will be strong, like a tree planted near water
that sends its roots by a stream.
It is not afraid when the days are hot;
its leaves are always green.
It does not worry in a year when no rain comes;
it always produces fruit."

JEREMIAH 17:8 NCV

The imagery here is stunning and memorable. It brings to mind John 4:13-15 and Revelation 21:6 where Jesus refers to himself as the living water. Think of yourself as the tree, and Jesus as the water in these verses. In order to live a vibrant, fruitful life, you need to be rooted in Christ.

You do not draw from outside resources (like the rain in this verse) for strength and sustenance; you draw from the living water. You do not fear outer circumstances that could wilt you (like the heat) because you draw from living water. You choose to find your support in Christ. Those who are rooted in Christ choose to prioritize the things that bring them into deeper relationship with him.

Move your focus from external fears, worries, and outward things, and prioritize your relationship with Jesus as your source.

EMERGING FROM DARKNESS

Lord, you give light to my lamp.
My God brightens the darkness around me.

Psalm 18:28 NCV

Do you ever feel like you can't feel God? Like you've lost sight of him somehow? Sometimes we aren't sure how to get back to that place where we feel his presence strongly and hear his voice clearly.

God will not push himself on you. He will not share his glory with another, and he will not try to compete with the world for your heart. But if you draw near to him, he will wrap you in the power of his presence. Welcome him into your life today. Ask him to be close. You won't always know where he is or what he is doing, but you can find him if you look.

Draw close to God today. Let his presence surround you in all that you do.

FEELING TRAPPED

The cords of the grave coiled around me;
the snares of death confronted me.

PSALM 18:5 NIV

This is our faith walk. While Jesus' light never goes out, sometimes our sight does. We get so bogged down by circumstances, by sin, by our own agendas, we can't see a thing.

So how do we keep moving? We cry out, and then we follow the sound of God's voice. We must step more slowly now, but we can still walk. We just need to listen and have faith in his voice. He is always ready to rescue you, but you have to acknowledge your distress first.

Ask God to rescue you. Know without a doubt that he hears your cries.

ASSURANCE OF ETERNITY

"I know that my Redeemer lives,
and he will stand upon the earth at last.
And after my body has decayed,
yet in my body I will see God! I will see him for myself.
Yes, I will see him with my own eyes.
I am overwhelmed at the thought!"

Job 19:25-27 NLT

In a matter of days, everything was destroyed. First his 11,000 livestock and servants were stolen, burned, or killed. Then his ten children all died at once. To make matters worse, this unfortunate man's skin was plagued with painful sores, which he scraped with a piece of broken pottery. How could anyone endure such tragedy?

To be fair, Job mourns, and laments, and weeps. He is confused, hopeless, and weak. On top of feeling cursed and desperate, he is taunted by his friends and wife: "Give up on God; he has given up on you!" Job's faith has been weakened by the test, but he clutched desperately to the one promise that could sustain him: no matter what happened to Job in his earth-bound life, nothing could take away the joy he would share with God in his eternal life.

Be assured of your eternal place in God's kingdom. Submit your life to Jesus Christ.

ADDRESS THE NEED

What good is it, dear brothers and sisters, if you say you have faith but don't show it by your actions? Can that kind of faith save anyone?

James 2:14 NLT

What is your faith worth? How far are you willing to go to express the love of God to a dying world? Will you give of yourself when it isn't convenient? Will you love on someone who is unlovable and give to someone who can never repay you?

The cost may seem great, and the work insignificant, but God sees your heart and what you have done, and he counts it as work done directly for him.

Show your faith in action toward those in need. As the Holy Spirit guides you to the needs of others, respond quickly.

VALUE OF FAITH

A brother or sister in Christ might need clothes or food. If you say to that person, "God be with you! I hope you stay warm and get plenty to eat," but you do not give what that person needs, your words are worth nothing

JAMES 2:15-16 NCV

As Christians, we are called to be the representation of Christ to the world; we are the visible expression of an invisible God. In order to express the heart of the Father, we have to know what is on his heart. God tells us in Scripture that he cares deeply about the least of these: the orphan, the widow, the poor, the foreigner.

We cannot preach Christ to someone who is needy while leaving them in their need. Our words will not communicate the love of our Father unless accompanied by the actions that make him tangible to them.

Think about how far you are willing to go to express the love of God to a dying world. Give of yourself when it isn't convenient.

HOLD ON

Stand firm and hold to the traditions that you were taught by us, either by our spoken word or by our letter.

2 THESSALONIANS 2:15 ESV

We are taught to remember grudges. Team loyalties inspire them. Political events, social faux pas, historic atrocities, and more vie to fill our brains with reasons we should be cross or judgmental. It is as though we are preserving an element of who we are—of tradition and identity—by strong-arming those who have blocked our joy.

Our truest identity, however, is hidden in Christ. Likewise, our crucial traditions are faith, hope, and love. Hold on to what matters. Let Christ sift through the rest. Get rid of the clutter in your heart and unload the baggage of earthly customs. Hold on to the traditions of heaven.

Restore one of God's teachings within you that has been displaced or needs strengthening. Read the Bible to gain new insight on it.

SUPPORTED

"Don't worry, because I am with you.
Don't be afraid, because I am your God.
I will make you strong and will help you;
I will support you with my right hand that saves you."

Isaiah 41:10 NCV

In our weakness, it is wise to lean on the support God provides. It is not failure to be helped; it is the reinforcement that causes us to be strengthened. When we think through those who have exhibited great faith, it isn't that they did great things on their own. That has never been the plot.

Abraham, Moses, Daniel, and Mary are a few examples of those who lived with perseverance. They also lived out incredible supernatural experiences, none of which were based on their own abilities. What are you facing right now that seems impossible? Is it as impossible as being thrown into a lion's den, or leaving for an unknown destination, or leading a nation of people into a desert?

Be encouraged today that your fear can turn to faith with God's mighty strength supporting you.

SOUL VACATION

"Are you weary, carrying a heavy burden? Come to me. I will refresh your life, for I am your oasis."

MATTHEW 11:28 TPT

The weeks leading up to a vacation may have you dreaming of a soft ocean breeze blowing in your hair and warm sun washing your body. Some days we just find ourselves longing for that vacation. Even the weekend looming ahead on a rough Wednesday morning seems like a great reprieve from life.

While vacations are a means to escape and find rest, they can never truly cure a weary soul. You could be lying on the beaches of Jamaica or freezing in an office in midwest America, and your weary soul would be your companion at both.

The only vacation destination for a weary soul is in the presence of Jesus. Find him and drink of the living water. Bask in the glory of a holy God. Rest in his arms of perfect love.

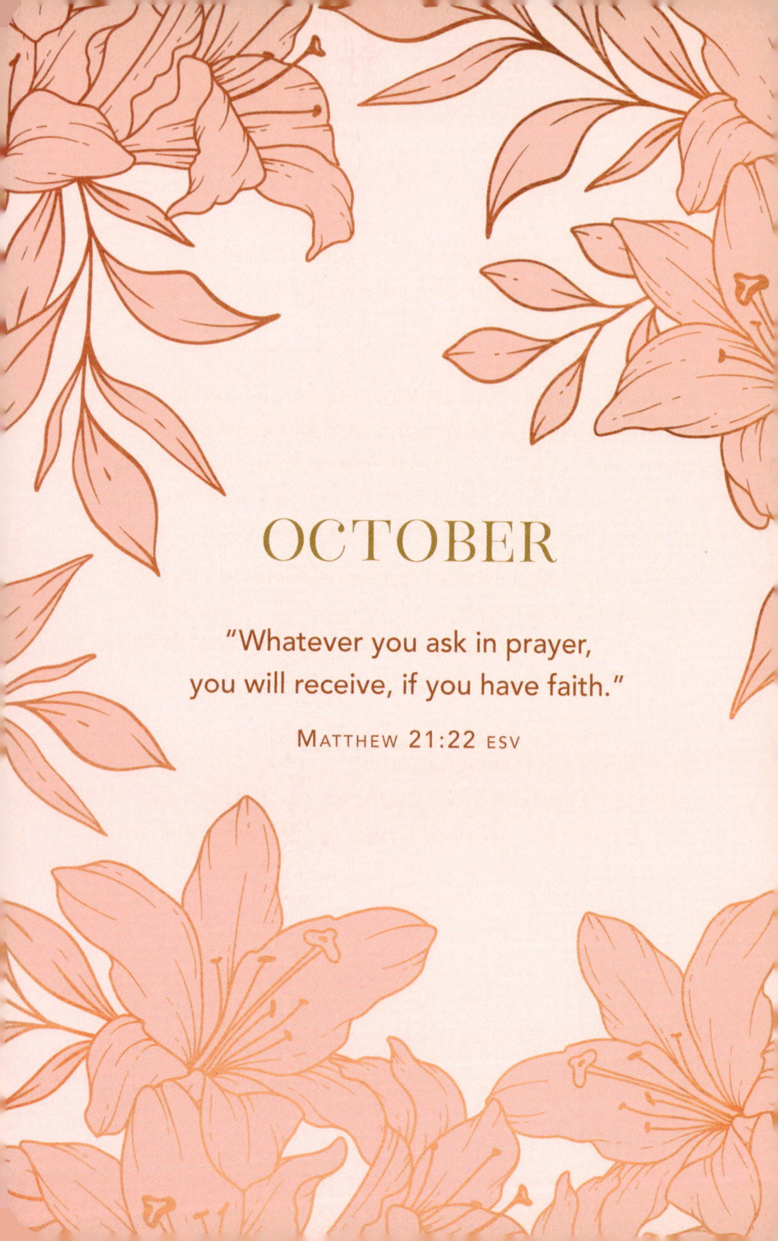

OCTOBER

"Whatever you ask in prayer,
you will receive, if you have faith."

MATTHEW 21:22 ESV

PROCLAIMING FAITH

May he give you the power to accomplish all the good things your faith prompts you to do.

2 THESSALONIANS 1:11 NLT

Have you ever been afraid of what others will think of you when they learn that you are a Christian? Do you ever worry that people may assume you are some sort of weirdo if you proclaim your faith? It can be hard enough to fit in without giving society another reason to shun you.

Be assured, there is no reason to be afraid! God has given us his Holy Spirit to guide us through tough conversations. Be bashful no more; he has equipped you with all the talent you need to share his love with those around you. There will be some who will laugh, and there will be some who will scorn you for your beliefs. God himself tells us through his Word that we have nothing to fear.

Shake off your timidity! Picture yourself shedding it like a winter coat in the warmth of spring. Be prepared to share your faith without fear. God has sent his Holy Spirit to give you power when you lack it. Take advantage of it!

MINDFUL DISCIPLINE

With your minds ready for action, be sober-minded and set your hope completely on the grace to be brought to you at the revelation of Jesus Christ.

1 Peter 1:13 CSB

Living by faith is not circumstantial, and it is not produced by accident. Faith is an active choosing to believe in something or someone. In the world of spirituality, discipline can get a bad rap. However, when we look into the practice of spiritual disciplines, they benefit our faith by training us to align to God's kingdom ways.

Have you been floating along in your faith, or have you been able to regulate your mind and actions in partnership with the Spirit? There is no condemnation or judgment for where you are today. Take hope in the grace that God freely gives to empower you to live liberated in his law of love. If you don't know where to begin, start by directing your heart toward him through his Word and through prayer.

Ask God to fill you with grace that gives you the strength to live aligned with his life and light. Expand the boundaries of your heart as you actively restrict where your attentions go.

FAITH EXPLANATION

I am not ashamed of this Good News about Christ. It is the power of God at work, saving everyone who believes—the Jew first and also the Gentile.

Romans 1:16 NLT

It can feel strange to be a Christian in this day and age; people are living their own truths. Although they may tolerate your faith, many believe there is not one right way, or they don't even care to know if there is a right thing to believe. Instead of fighting this philosophy and mentality, make some effort to explain your faith in a way that is meaningful in today's context.

No one can argue with your personal experience of knowing Christ and having a certain peace with knowing the promise for your future. If you get a chance this week to mention your faith, be brave and not ashamed of the gospel that has freed you and can free others.

Look for opportunities where you can share your personal experience of knowing Christ with someone. Think of all that you have been blessed with and start giving God the glory for those things.

UNSTAINED

Pure and undefiled religion in the sight of our God and Father is this: to visit orphans and widows in their distress, and to keep oneself unstained by the world.

JAMES 1:27 NASB

Simply calling ourselves Christians, attending church, and participating in religious activities does not make us followers of Jesus. Following Jesus and living as he lived is what defines true faith. When we begin to act the way God tells us to, we will look different from those around us.

We are part of this world, but we are of a different kingdom. Our pursuits are considered as having little importance to the world. Rather than pursue riches, we seek to help the distressed. Instead of taking care of ourselves, we take care of others.

Ask God to lead you to those who are in need of help. Keep your eyes open to the oppressed and destitute. Reorient your values and live by the laws of God's kingdom rather than appeasing the world's insatiable wants.

INFLUENCERS

I am reminded of your sincere faith, a faith that dwelt first in your grandmother Lois and your mother Eunice and now, I am sure, dwells in you as well.

2 Timothy 1:5 ESV

Who are Lois and Eunice? From this verse, we can gather that they are the grandmother and mother of Timothy. If this verse had been omitted from the Bible, however, you would never know. They don't have a book of the Bible named after them. They probably didn't go on any missionary journeys. But this sentence about them speaks volumes. They had faith, and they taught this faith to their children. They discipled Timothy in the faith of Christ, and he went on to preach the gospel and fulfill his calling. Without Lois and Eunice, would there be a Timothy? Would Paul have written two letters to encourage him?

You cannot fathom the great things God wants to do with what you think is your small circle of influence. Be faithful in the small, and God will bless it. You are called to share the gospel and live out your faith, whether you disciple one person or millions. Maybe you only ever see your kids, grandkids, nieces, or nephews. It matters. Your influence matters.

Ask God to remind you of the impact of your spiritual influence. Whose life can you speak into today?

ADD TO FAITH

Make every effort to add to your faith goodness; and to goodness, knowledge; and to knowledge, self-control; and to self-control, perseverance; and to perseverance, godliness; and to godliness, mutual affection; and to mutual affection, love.

2 PETER 1:5-7 NIV

If you see this list of virtues as a checklist, then you are looking at it the wrong way. You know that God isn't about a list of right things to do. Instead look simply at where it all starts: with faith.

When you build your faith through reading God's Word and spending time in his presence, you will notice the other virtues begin to be added to your faith. With belief comes goodness, knowledge, and self-control. Where is your faith right now? Remind yourself of your salvation through belief in Christ, and let the rest work itself out from there.

Your belief in Jesus is what saves you, not all the good or right things that you do. Ask God to build those other characteristics as your faith increases. Ask for me knowledge, self-control, godliness, and love.

PRICELESS FAITH

These troubles come to prove that your faith is pure. This purity of faith is worth more than gold, which can be proved to be pure by fire but will ruin. But the purity of your faith will bring you praise and glory and honor when Jesus Christ is shown to you.

1 Peter 1:7 NCV

In difficult times, it's tempting to sink into questioning. We want to know why. Most of the answers are not ours to know on this side of heaven, but Scripture can provide powerful encouragement while we wait. Gold is so precious it was once a universal standard for measuring wealth, yet, according to this verse, faith that remains strong through adversity is even more valuable. Such faith is priceless.

Regardless of the struggles we face, when we keep hold of our faith, we gain a glorious reward: the praise, honor and glory of Christ the King. Faith that withstands the fire of adversity brings blessings beyond all imagining.

Invite God to use your pain, both now and in the future, to test and prove your faith. Understand that a struggle that deepens your trust in him is a struggle worth enduring, and sorrow that increases your comprehension of his goodness is sorrow you can face.

FAITH BEFORE SIGHT

Though you have not seen him, you love him. Though you do not now see him, you believe in him and rejoice with joy that is inexpressible and filled with glory, obtaining the outcome of your faith, the salvation of your souls.

1 Peter 1:8-9 ESV

The longer we walk with the Lord, the more we appreciate and enjoy his salvation and his unending companionship. Jesus' faithfulness is a cornerstone for our own faith in him. We know we can trust him because he has proven himself trustworthy.

One day, you will reach a point where you need to know God is real in your own situation. You won't be able to look at him physically. You won't be able to call and hear his audible voice, perhaps. But you will know, from past experience, that he knows you intimately and is there for you. There is not a thing you face, not a thought that crosses your mind, that God hasn't dealt with yet. He is there for you. You can trust him.

The unseen is more tangible, eternally, than the visible. Place your faith in Jesus to become eternally tangible.

HEARING GOD

So faith comes from hearing,
and hearing through the word of Christ.

Romans 10:17 ESV

The best way to know if something is true or right is to hear it for yourself—straight from the source. You believe you nailed the interview, but you don't believe you got the job until you get the phone call. You think you might have aced the test, but you wait for the results before telling anyone. The same is true for bad news—ideally. You get wind of a rumor about a friend's indiscretion, but you wait for their side of the story before believing a word.

So what about God? How can we hear from him? How do we discern his will for our lives? We may not have a hotline, but we do have his book. God speaks to us through his Word, so if you are waiting for confirmation, direction, validation, or conviction, pick it up. Read it. And listen.

God can speak to you through his Word. Are your conversations as frequent and meaningful as you'd like? Share your heart with him right now and listen for his reply.

LOOKING FOR LABORERS

"The harvest is plentiful, but the workers are few. Ask the Lord of the harvest, therefore, to send out workers into his harvest field."

LUKE 10:2 NIV

Roy could tell that this year was going to yield the best harvest he'd ever had. The peach tree limbs were drooping from the weight of the fruit. There was a bumper crop of beans, corn, and squash, and there would be hundreds of bushels of tomatoes to send to the market. You'd think he would be excited, and he was, but his biggest emotion was worry. The Farmer's Almanac predicted major storms for the next few weeks, the kind that would bring heavy winds and hail that would ruin the crops. He and his family had spent long days in the fields, but they weren't making a dent with all that needed to be harvested. He was looking for laborers, but couldn't get the responses he needed.

God is also looking for good workers. There are people all over the world who are waiting for someone to bring them the gospel—a harvest of souls for God—but so few people answer the call. Will you be one of his laborers today?

There is a plentiful harvest of souls around you. You can be one of God's laborers by sharing the good news with someone today.

ACKNOWLEDGE

"Whoever acknowledges me before others, I will also acknowledge them before my Father in heaven."

MATTHEW 10:32 NIV

Have you ever been at a party where the host is making introductions and when it comes to you, your name slips their mind? It is embarrassing. No one likes to be forgotten. It does not have to cause an offense, yet you worry that possibly you were an afterthought, or that the host was pressured to include you.

Someday, we will all stand before the Father, and he will open the book of life. The ultimate lack of acknowledgment would be if Jesus turned to the Father and said, "This one is not mine. Depart from me; I never knew you." At that point, it will be too late. You won't have the option to explain your decision to neglect accepting the Savior during your earthly life. You won't be able to excuse not speaking his glorious name to win others to him. The die will be cast.

Today you have time. You have a choice. Align yourself with the name and life of Jesus, and he will do the same for you. Share your faith in Jesus with someone today.

KEEP THE FAITH

Do not throw away this confident trust in the Lord. Remember the great reward it brings you!

HEBREWS 10:35 NLT

Have you ever waivered in your faith? Was there a time when you felt that living for God was just too hard? Perhaps he seemed distant and unhearing. Many Christians across the ages have felt just like that. Even giants in Christian history have had their doubts. C.S. Lewis concluded there was no God in his early adulthood, finally coming back full circle to not just believing but spending the rest of his life writing and lecturing about Jesus. Millions have read his books.

God loves you. He understands what you are going through. He knows you have doubts. He wants to remind you that this time is fleeting. Put your trust in him and get through this hard situation. God is always there listening to you. There is great treasure awaiting you. Be brave, be fearless, have courage, and continue to trust the Lord who guards your heart.

Even though it may seem God is far away at times, he never is. Listen for his voice today and renew your devotion to him. When you are low, ask for encouragement and believe he will send it.

SEEK HIM OUT

Seek more of his strength! Seek more of him!
Let's always be seeking the light of his face.

Psalm 105:4 TPT

If only we could carry the feeling we get from a great church service, Bible study, concert, or conference everywhere we go. When we are filled with the Spirit, God's strength is our strength. When we are inspired by praise, we see the world through the Lord's eyes. When open to his amazing power, our wounds can be healed. How pleasant it would be to continuously seek more of him and bask in his light.

Life tends to make continual basking impossible, though. We have bills to pay, tests to study for, and things to clean. We are worn down by stress. These all distract us from seeking God. Having wandered from that wonderful place, the place we felt him closer than our own skin, we are reminded of how much we crave it—how much we need it. We're reminded to seek, to search, to pursue his presence. When we can't feel his light, we need only turn toward his face. Arms open, he's right where we left him.

If you've wandered away from your closeness with God, come back. Find him in the obvious places where love, light, and life are present.

NO HOLDING BACK

Go ahead—let everyone know it!
Tell the world how he broke through and delivered you from the power of darkness and has gathered us together from all over the world.
He has set us free to be his very own!

PSALM 107:2 TPT

How many people know the story of how you first fell in love with Jesus? How many are aware of the intimacy you share with him: the nudges, the whispers, and the dreams? Let nothing hold you back. Imagine your life without him and realize the importance of sharing the amazing truth of how you came to live with him.

Maybe because your story is so familiar to you, you've never thought of it as important enough to share, or as something everyone needs to know. But everyone does need to know God. They need to hear your experience of discovering his perfect love and saving truth. It might help someone else meet him, and that should fill you with a new sense of urgency to make sure they hear all about him.

Write down your faith story. Whether a paragraph or several volumes, write it out and be prepared to share it with others.

CONSISTENT HOPE

May the God of hope fill you with all joy and peace as you believe so that you may overflow with hope by the power of the Holy Spirit.

ROMANS 15:13 CSB

Hope. it is whispered in the budding on bare branches after a long winter. It races through the droplets set free from the ice, melted down and moving once again. Experience it in the shifting of the wind across your face from a painful slap of cold to a gentle caress of warmth. The brilliant colors of the tulips shout it loud as our monochromatic world has the saturation turned up. The chorus of birds out again sing in harmony: hope. The season of spring brings us a reminder of what we are to be filled with daily.

In Christ, there is no such thing as false hope. There is only unshakeable, unmovable, constant, abundant, hope. All the temporary things will rust, rot, and be lost in the age to come. Our anchor lies in the fact that Christ is coming back, he has prepared a place for us, he will wipe away every tear, and make new all things once more. If hope seems lost, readjust to an eternal mindset, and watch it bloom once again.

In what way has your hope been set on the wrong thing, and how can you adjust?

CONFIDENT FAITH

Faith is confidence in what we hope for and assurance about what we do not see.

HEBREWS 11:1 NIV

The word *faith* can seem so abstract. It's a word you paint in calligraphy and hang on signs in your house, yet it feels a little ambiguous. What does this verse mean? To have faith in God is to stand confidently and take as fact that God exists and he is at work even if we can't see him at work. Our faith doesn't have to stay the same.

If you struggle with the concept of faith as well, take heart that you can grow in it over time. It is a gift from God: step one is asking for it! Step two is acknowledging that you don't have to settle for the same amount of faith you've always had. Ask for more. Step three, let your faith be developed by trusting in God's ways. The ways you can see, and the ways that leave you with whys. All of these steps rely on God.

Faith is for the wonderful seasons and downright challenging ones alike. Ask God today to fill you confidently with faith.

CONVICTION

Let us draw near with a true heart in full assurance of faith, with our hearts sprinkled clean from an evil conscience and our bodies washed with pure water.

HEBREWS 10:22 ESV

Hebrews 11 is known as the faith chapter in the Bible. It recalls those who lived their lives tenaciously clinging to the promises of God especially when those promises were far off and it was not clear how God would fulfill them. We have the hindsight of history that oversimplifies the process from promise to fulfillment. However, when we consider the humanity of the founders of our faith, we can see the same threads that ran through their lives run through ours.

They faced uncertainty and trials of many kinds although different than those we face. May we echo the faith they clung to, believing that the same God who came through for them will also come through for us. He is faithful to his Word and to his people. May our conviction in God's goodness run deeper than the doubts that shifting circumstances bring.

God is always faithful. His character doesn't change. You can take courage in the the testimonies of those who have walked with him before you.

FAITH IS CONFIDENT

God did this so that, by two unchangeable things in which it is impossible for God to lie, we who have fled to take hold of the hope set before us may be greatly encouraged.

HEBREWS 6:18 NIV

Our hope in Christ is not a wish or a gamble. We are confident that things will happen exactly as the Bible predicts them. We have a hope so certain it leads directly to our faith. We do not need to see the future to know the end of the story, because everything has happened to this point exactly as God detailed that it would.

We have faith in the unseen, but not the unknown, because we know God. He has proven himself and his character over and over again for as long as we have existed. Because of him, we have faith to follow him confidently into the future. Our faith is not simply a verbal confession. It is an active and obedient way of living that proves we hope in the Lord.

Although you have not seen the future, you can know who God is. Throughout the recorded Scriptures, he has proven that he is loving, faithful, and true. For this reason, you do not need to fear the future.

YOURS

This is the reason I urge you to boldly believe for whatever you ask for in prayer—be convinced that you have received it and it will be yours.

MARK 11:24 TPT

Faith is confidence. Do you usually associate confidence with pride? That's because the world shows us that confidence comes from pridefully putting our trust in ourselves. It is a selfish ambition only when the source is yourself. But children of God are called to be confident, and it's actually humble to do so! Confidence is trusting in Jesus.

You have the assurance of who Jesus is and who you are to him. Your identity is completely wrapped up in him, and with Jesus as your source, you can walk out your days full of faith displayed for all to see. The power comes from the one who lives inside of you. Dare to live with faith and confidence today.

Be filled with new faith! Ask God boldy for what you need and trust him to come through for you.

BECAUSE WE KNOW

Through his creative inspiration
this Living Expression made all things,
for nothing has existence apart from him!

JOHN 1:3 TPT

Could you prove creation in a court of law? Could you prove the Creator? What physical evidence do you have to back up your faith? And yet, could you deny him? Could you deny what, by faith, you know to be true? Faith is a beautiful mystery. While proof exists in the physical world, faith lives in the heart. We know what we know simply because we know. The instant the Father called us to him, all that was speculation became truth.

Once we get past childhood, we typically need to see in order to believe. Hearing that out of nothing that can be seen came everything we see, skepticism is not a surprising response. But for faith, we'd never move past it. Look at those first three words: faith empowers us. Without faith, believing God created the universe—believing he exists at all—isn't just a stretch; it's impossible.

You can have more faith in God than everything you can prove. Have you been changed by his Word, healed by his love, or felt his presence in your soul? All of that should be proof enough.

BUILDING FAITH

Faith empowers us to see that the universe was created and beautifully coordinated by the power of God's words! He spoke and the invisible realm gave birth to all that is seen.

HEBREWS 11:3 TPT

Faith can be a difficult, abstract concept. What are we really saying when we say we have faith? At the beginning of Hebrews 11, we are not told what faith is, but rather what faith does. It fortifies what we hope for. It is the foundation of our relationship with God. When you are building, you start with a foundation and work your way up, much like God started with nothing and built the heavens and the earth with his spoken Word. We start with faith, the belief of Jesus Christ's work on the cross.

But it doesn't stop there! Your faith should continue to build from belief into confidence as you enter into a deeper relationship. As your relationship matures, confidence deepens trust. Different aspects of faith can be at different levels, for the character of God is vast and unmeasurable. You can trust that he is good while just beginning to believe that he is just.

Is there an aspect of the character of God that evades your hope? By faith, take hold of your ability to rightly understand that aspect.

OUT OF NOTHING

By the word of the LORD the heavens were made,
their starry host by the breath of his mouth.

PSALM 33:6 NIV

As Christians, we believe that God created the universe with just the power of his word. Everything he made, he made to be beautiful and to bring him glory. God's power goes beyond our comprehension. He did not need existing materials to change and shape into what he wanted; all he had to do was speak the world into existence, and it was.

God speaks incredible things into being, even when we cannot see their origin. We may not see the ways God works in our lives, but God reveals to us just what we need to know at exactly the right time. His wisdom is perfect, and we can trust that wisdom. Our faith is all he asks for in return.

God's power is high above your words. Praise him for using it for the good of those who love him. Trust him through the process of figuring out his plan for your life.

ALL ABOUT GOD

From him and through him and for him are all things.
To him be the glory forever. Amen!

ROMANS 11:36 NIV

"She is very religious; she's always talking about God!" What was meant as an insult was really quite a compliment. Has this ever been said about you? Maybe it has, and it shut you up. With cheeks flushed, you felt judged and misread by the person you were with. Do not be ashamed. What some meant as harm is really a reflection of the gift God has given you. If you have tunnel vision for Jesus, you are not on the wrong path. The Bible, and this verse in Romans, makes it pretty clear that we are to be all about the kingdom of God!

We are not called to live in a divide of the sacred and the secular, but in all things give God the glory. Not everyone will understand why you choose to make God your happy place and bring him up in areas they don't think he belongs. Don't mind them. You are not too much; God loves how you can see him in all the details of life.

Make a point to see God in all things instead of dividing sacred and secular. His glory can be seen everywhere; you only have to look for it.

NO OFFENSE

"Blessed is the one who isn't offended by me."

Matthew 11:6 CSB

Many days we may catch ourselves wondering where God is. In the middle of all the chaos and loud opinions, sometimes faith in Christ seems absurd. We feel a form of persecution in the world when we hear others laugh about Christianity or find a way to blame religion for all the wrong.

To the world, the message of the cross is offensive. To those who believe, the message of Christ is true fulfilment because it is a message full of hope, peace, and joy. We may not understand why we believe all that we do about God, but we must know that he can handle our doubt. He can restore unwavering faith and show us that we are living in the truth.

If you have moments of feeling like your faith has taken a knock, you are not alone! Take your doubt and uncertainty to God and ask him to help you.

MOUNTAIN MOVERS

"If anyone says to this mountain, 'Go throw yourself into the sea,' and does not doubt in their heart but believes that what they say will happen, it will be done for them."

MARK 11:23 NIV

Matthew 17:20 tells us that if we have faith as small as a mustard seed, we can move mountains. Since none of us have plans to pick up Mount Kilimanjaro and find a new spot for it, how can we apply this knowledge to our own lives? Truly, it sounds a bit wacky that we can do great things with only a little faith. And yet Scripture tells us that it's so!

How can we step out in faith? It looks different for everyone. For some, the first step may be giving themselves fully to a belief that Christ died for their sins. For others, it could look like jumping out of a job that isn't a good fit and taking a leap into the unknown, or giving up a toxic relationship knowing that the Lord will be there to take care of them.

Take a leap of faith today. Reflect on what that looks like for you and get ready to be rewarded when you step out.

EARNESTLY SEEK

Without faith it is impossible to please God, because anyone who comes to him must believe that he exists and that he rewards those who earnestly seek him.

HEBREWS 11:6 NIV

If you went to summer camp as a kid or teenager, you probably have fond memories of the activities. From campfires to meals in the cafeteria, you made new friendships and strengthened old ones. There may have been a team-building time that included a trust fall. That is when you let go of your body and fall backwards, believing that the person behind you will catch you and not allow you to end up in the dirt.

Hebrews tells us that without faith, we cannot please God. If we are going to make a request of him, we need to believe that he will answer us. We must acknowledge his character, that he is an all-powerful God that keeps his word. If we doubt what the Word tells us, we are like a wave of the sea, thrown here and there by the wind, and we should not expect anything from the Lord. And when we receive our answer, we must remember that even if it differs from what we wanted, our wise and loving heavenly Father has answered in a way that is best for us.

When you pray today, make it a prayer full of faith, pleasing to the Lord.

FAITH WITHOUT SIGHT

It was by faith that Abraham obeyed when God called him to leave home and go to another land that God would give him as his inheritance. He went without knowing where he was going.

HEBREWS 11:8 NLT

Abraham, the father of the faithful, was a man of obedience. Had he heard God's call but disregarded it out of fear or disbelief, God could not have established a new nation through his descendants. Abraham took the risk because he was convinced that God was true, and he set out for a place he did not know. Genuine faith always obeys God. In fact, our obedience to God is the indication that our faith is real. Abraham took one step at a time before the next step was revealed.

This morning you may be following the Lord as though you are in the dark. You just don't see where he is leading you. Remember that he sees the entire picture and is engineering the circumstances of your life very carefully. He knows what he is doing, and he asks that you take just one step of faith at a time.

Reaffirm your faith in God today. Remember that he is good and faithful and that he loves you too much to leave you directionless.

STEADY HEARTS

They won't be afraid of bad news;
their hearts are steady because they trust the LORD.

PSALM 112:7 NCV

None of us like to receive bad news, but we do not live in dread of it like those whose security is shaky. Our hope is rooted in our steadfast Lord, and our confidence comes from knowing him. We cannot secure our own futures nor the results of certain circumstances. In the end, we know the final conclusion of all things is our victory through Christ.

God knows the future and has a perfect plan in place. He is not surprised by sudden disappointments; he has been preparing us to handle them. For this reason, we do not live in fear but in freedom. Our hearts are steady because we trust God, and he has given us his peace.

Your heart can know peace because you know God. Focus on keeping your heart steady and not anxious about things you cannot predict or control.

IDOLS

Their idols are merely things of silver and gold,
shaped by human hands.

PSALM 115:4 NLT

It's important to understand that not everyone will choose to the serve the Lord. We live in a world that has temptations that some will not be able to resist. We live in a world where we may be mocked for our decision to follow the Lord. Yet it is important to make a decision one way or another just as Joshua did. As Scripture says, we cannot serve two masters.

When you make the choice, be brave and bold about choosing to follow God. Don't chase other things that will never bring true joy to your heart. You will only ever be satisfied with a choice to leave other idols behind and follow God.

Make God your number one choice today and serve him fully.

CHILDLIKE IN FAITH

The LORD protects those of childlike faith;
I was facing death, and he saved me.

PSALM 116:6 NLT

Being childlike is different than being childish. Young children are generally teachable, unassuming, and trusting. God's favor rests on those who humble themselves like a child (Matthew 18:3-4). He wants us to depend on him completely just as children possess a carefree dependence on their parents.

When we come to the end of ourselves and acknowledge our weakness, we are then able to receive the help that the Lord longs to give us. He takes delight in caring for us, his beloved children. Isaiah 42:3 says he will not break a bruised reed. None of us are so broken as to be beyond hope. He will not leave us defenseless; he will come to our aid.

Think of all the times you have seen God show himself as faithful in times of trouble. Remember that when you feel weak, you can depend on him to give you strength.

SAFE IN HIM

The LORD is for me; he will help me.
It is better to take refuge in the LORD
than to trust in people.

PSALM 118:7-8 NLT

There is a new scam every minute. Mail fraud, internet con, and theft are frequently on the news. People let you down. It is difficult to have confidence in others because we may be disappointed. We need to put our ultimate faith in the Lord.

When someone misses a deadline, we can trust God to have our backs. He can help us in any situation. The Lord will never break a confidence. He is a safe place to unburden our thoughts. We can trust him with our finances and our career questions. God cherishes our hopes and dreams and offers wise counsel. Take refuge in his care for you.

When you have questions, take refuge in God. He will guide you, counsel you, and give you advice. Your innermost thoughts and dreams are safe with him.

NOVEMBER

"Don't let your hearts be troubled.
Trust in God, and trust also in me."

John 14:1 NLT

THE PERFECT PATTERN

I want you to pattern your lives after me, just as I pattern mine after Christ.

1 Corinthians 11:1 TPT

When constructing a garment, you could try to make it just by guessing and cutting. However, most good seamstresses follow a pattern. Patterns are thin sheets of paper that you lay over your fabric, using their shapes to cut out the fabric exactly how you need it. If you follow the pattern, you can be fairly sure the outcome will look like what you were hoping.

In the same manner, Paul wrote this verse to the church in Corinthians. He patterned his life after Christ, so they could pattern their lives after him. If we attempt to wing it, we are going to end up with a pretty messed up garment. We could also pattern our lives after the world, but then we will end up sharing the world's fate. As Christians, the best way to live a life that brings glory to God is to pattern your life after Christ.

What or who are you patterning your life after? Ask God to help you keep the worldly patterns out so you can bring glory to him.

HEALING POWER

"I will bring it health and healing;
I will heal them and reveal to them
the abundance of peace and truth."

JEREMIAH 33:6 NKJV

Have you heard of the marvelous works that God has done? If you need healing, emotionally, spiritually, relationally, or physically, turn to your Bible to find testimony of our God who heals. Making things new is what he does, and he does not want you to stay stuck in the brokenness you are experiencing.

As you find accounts of the blind seeing, the lame walking, and the dead coming alive again, let them encourage your soul. He is not done doing these things. The work he did in Jeremiah's time of restoration, the work he did in the lives of so many throughout the Bible, is not a closed case. His healing power is alive for you today.

Find encouragement from the testimonies in Scripture and let faith arise in you.

SOIL OF HIS LOVE

They quickly shot up, but when the days grew hot, they were scorched and withered because they had insufficient roots.

MATTHEW 13:5-6 TPT

Do you want your faith to grow strong? Do you want gratitude to spill out of you for all that the Lord is and does? Then let the roots of your life grow in the soil of Jesus' love. You can never exaggerate the love of God. You will not spoil his goodness. Build your life upon his character, for he is faithful. When you are standing on the truth of God's Word, revealed through Jesus, you will not fall.

Let Jesus lead you in his mercy today. Meditate on his Word. Allow him to speak into your life. Look for his goodness in the mundane. Keep an open line of prayer throughout the day. Give him access to your thoughts, to your heart, and surrender to his leading.

Jesus is trustworthy and he knows how to take care of you. Let your roots grow deep in him.

NOT IN VAIN

Be firm, immovable, always excelling in the work of the Lord, knowing that your labor is not in vain in the Lord.

1 CORINTHIANS 15:58 NASB

The hope we have in Jesus is incomparable to any hope we could have in this world or its systems. God will never fail to faithfully follow through on his promises. He will always offer us the mercy of his heart when we look for him. May our hearts remain steadfastly focused on Jesus, the author and finisher of our faith. In him, our faith originates, for he calls us to himself. And in him, our faith is perfected, for he is the one who has makes us right with God.

Do you have an answer for the hope of your faith? Take some time to consider how you would respond to someone who asks you the reason you hope in God. Open up a prayerful conversation with Jesus and ask for his insight. And remember, with gentleness and respect, we reflect the love of Jesus.

There is no need to be forceful; just authentically reflect how God has changed you. There is no perfect or right way to do it. It will not be in vain if you are doing it for the Lord.

SPRINGS OF LIVING WATER

"The Lamb in the midst of the throne will be their shepherd, and he will guide them to springs of living water, and God will wipe away every tear from their eyes."

REVELATION 7:17 ESV

Jesus guides us to springs of living water, and he calms our fears. One day, when his kingdom comes in its fullness, with Jesus leading the way, every wrong will be made right, and every fear will be forever settled. He will wipe every tear from our eyes. There will be no more pain and no more sorrow.

Until that day, Jesus meets us in our pain. He fills us with the refreshing waters of his presence. He comforts us in our grief, and he settles our fears with his peace. The Holy Spirit ministers to us now, and it is a glimpse of what is to come. We walk by faith for now, not by sight. But someday, everything will be clear. We will see him face to face. We will behold him as clearly as we see our families and friends.

He will shine brighter than the sun in all its glory, and you will not be blinded. What a marvelous day to look forward to!

WAY OF THE GOOD

You will walk in the way of the good
and keep to the paths of the righteous.
For the upright will inhabit the land,
and those with integrity will remain in it.

PROVERBS 2:20-21 ESV

Whatever we are facing, no matter what struggles or challenges, there is a clear vision for us to focus on—Jesus. He is the pioneer of our faith. Having gone before us, he paved the path we take to the Father.

Where we have become distracted and confused, let us refocus today on Jesus. There is no one worthy of a place above him. No one can match his mercy, his faithfulness, or his might. We can look to him for the way to go, how to proceed, and for all that we need. He leads us into the fullness of God's kingdom, here and now.

Through fellowship with the Spirit, you receive the abundance of his grace and mercy, and you have access to the power of God in your life.

NOTHING IMPOSSIBLE

"I know that You can do everything,
And that no purpose of Yours can be withheld from You."

Job 42:2 NKJV

How often do we live with faith propelling us into the great unknown, full of possibilities and goodness? Are we growing in the grace of God, stepping outside of what we have known into the deeper waters of confidence in God's power? His love is not stagnant; it is always moving. It is a rushing river and a tidal wave, tearing down our defenses and the limitations of what we have known.

God cannot be restricted to our experience. He will not be put in a box according to our understanding. He is outside of it. He dwells in the realm where nothing is impossible. As we know him more, our faith stretches. May we not stay in our comfortable boxes of comprehension. Yesterday's revelation is a building block, but it is not a full structure to build our lives upon.

God is always greater than you can fathom, so press into the mystery to know him better and expand your faith.

BEAUTIFUL MYSTERY

This message was kept secret for centuries and generations past, but now it has been revealed to God's people. For God wanted them to know that the riches and glory of Christ are for you Gentiles, too. And this is the secret: Christ lives in you. This gives you assurance of sharing his glory.

COLOSSIANS 1:26-27 NLT

In the ups and downs of life, if we are to trust God more than we trust ourselves, we must believe that he is as good as his Word describes. Jesus is as real today as he was when he walked the earth. He is living in the presence of the Father, and his resurrection life holds power for all who believe in him.

Jesus himself said that those who have not seen him and yet believe in him are blessed. Though we have not touched him, his power still moves in our lives. Though we have not studied his features, his gaze is full of lovingkindness as he looks at us. Though we have not witnessed the miracles he did while walking this earth, we still see his mercy on display today.

Press, with hope, into the tangible presence of the Holy Spirit. Though you do not see Jesus, you can know him. What a beautiful mystery!

NO GREATER LAW

"'Love the Lord your God with all your heart and with all your soul and with all your mind and with all your strength.' The second is this: 'Love your neighbor as yourself.' There is no commandment greater than these."

MARK 12:30-31 NIV

The law of love is so simple. It distills all the Old Testament laws into the overarching directive of God's heart and purposes. When we live out love, choosing to bolster the well-being of others as we would have them do for us, we reflect the kindness of God. Jesus did not add or take away from what God had revealed up until the point of his ministry. He fulfilled it, confirming the simple and profound motivation behind it all.

When we don't know what to do or how to proceed in a matter, let us come back to the foundation of our faith. May we choose to love God with all our hearts, souls, minds, and strength, in all that we do and say.

Display love that lays down its preferences for the good of another, a love that sticks up for the defenseless and feeds the poor. There is no law against this kind of love.

APPROPRIATE STANDARDS

In those days Israel had no king; everyone did as they saw fit.

JUDGES 21:25 NIV

This short phrase from the book of Judges speaks volumes about the state of the culture of God's chosen people during that time. The standard for what was deemed good was reduced to whatever a person felt was appropriate for them. Driven by their sinful natures, some of the more horrific stories in the Bible follow in the book of Judges. A people left to their own devices will bend toward their sinful nature, twisting and mutilating truth until it is unrecognizable.

With our current culture screaming for everyone to follow their own truth, the familiarity to the Judges passage is eerie. As children of God, we know better. We have the solid, unshakeable, unchanging Word of God to root our lives. The Word of God tells us what is appropriate for life and what is not. We must adopt his standard as our own standard for truth if we desire to live a life that glorifies Christ.

Examine yourself today. In what ways are you adopting the attitude and lifestyle of what is right in your eyes, instead of humbly asking God what is right in his eyes?

PURSUIT

"Well did Isaiah prophesy of you hypocrites, as it is written, 'This people honors me with their lips, but their heart is far from me; in vain do they worship me, teaching as doctrines the commandments of men.' You leave the commandment of God and hold to the tradition of men."

MARK 7:6-8 ESV

When we become believers, we get to know God better through study of his Word and prayer. This leads some to pursue higher education in the Bible, known as the study of theology. For those that don't go that route, there is still an abundance of books by Christian authors, pastors, and teachers on all areas of knowledge about God.

These resources in and of themselves are not bad, and many can be helpful to our growth. However, in our quest to gain knowledge of God, let us not lose the intimacy of a relationship with God. Striving to be informed is not a bad pursuit, but like many pursuits, it can become an idol. In a marriage, if you only focus on facts about a person, you are more of a biographer and less of a lover. To have intimacy, one must pursue experience, give time, and express vulnerability.

Don't forget that you are not just participating in a religion of research. You are pursuing a relationship with the God of creation.

LEGACY OF JESUS

We will not hide these truths from our children;
we will tell the next generation
about the glorious deeds of the LORD,
about his power and his mighty wonders.

PSALM 78:4 NLT

When considering legacy, many people focus on material possessions or their life's work. As Christians, the legacy we should seek is that people would say they know we treasured Jesus more than anything else.

We have an enemy, Satan, whose purpose is to steal, kill, and destroy. He wants nothing more than to steal this legacy from us and destroy any testimony we have. We must be careful keepers of our legacy. It is helpful to step back and look at our lives. What would your friends or family say you treasure most? Your phone? Your career? Your pets or home decor? How are you using your assets and time? What occupies your thought life the most? These self-evaluating questions can help you see if Jesus is your legacy, or if you've been deceived.

Prayerfully consider the questions listed above and evaluate your current legacy.

HAVE FAITH

When Jesus heard this, He responded to him, "Do no be afraid any longer, only believe, and she will be made well."

LUKE 8:50 NASB

Doubt is not the opposite of faith; fear is. This can be difficult to remember during hard times. Fear can manifest itself in our lives in many ways. When we get on the treadmill of worry, we give in to fear. When we try desperately to grasp for control, we let fear have that control. Many times in his ministry, Jesus tells people to not be afraid, to not worry, and to have faith.

What does worry do? What does it accomplish? Deep down, we all know that it accomplishes nothing. Faith turns our worries into prayers, entrusting those worries to the one who can do something about them. The disciples felt out of control several times in their time with Jesus. Think about the stories of the thousands who needed to be fed, or the giant waves that plummeted their boats. Jesus didn't ask them to take control of the situation. He just asked that they have faith in him.

Anxiety may look like frantically searching for answers, finding a different area you can control and hyper-focusing on that, or lashing out in relationships. Instead of choosing fear, choose faith.

CREDIT

The words "it was credited to him" were written not for him alone, but also for us, to whom God will credit righteousness—for us who believe in him who raised Jesus our Lord from the dead. He was delivered over to death for our sins and was raised to life for our justification.

ROMANS 4:23-24 NIV

Have you ever read a book that felt like it was written just for you? Perhaps it was a grand fiction tale with such vivid characters that you could see yourself in one of them. Maybe it was a memoir written by a person whose experience was so familiar, it could have been your own. Paul tells us here that something that was written long ago about Abraham's life was not just for him. It was written for you!

You can put yourself into this story. The abundant credit of righteousness that Abraham received as a result of his faith is for you too. If you have confessed Christ as Lord and believe in his resurrection and your subsequent justification, then the righteousness of God is yours. It covers you. When God looks at you, he sees the righteousness of Christ.

The payment has been made, and your debt is credited in full. The balance doesn't just rest at zero. You are given infinitely more because his righteousness is that rich.

SATISFACTION

Jesus said to them, "I am the bread of life; whoever comes to me shall not hunger, and whoever believes in me shall never thirst."

JOHN 6:35 ESV

Every person in the world wants to know what will make them happy. There are books written about it, conferences and seminars on it, and we all often go on the quest to find our happiness. From our childhood, we look for things that will bring us pleasure. We long for things that will bring us accomplishment, people who will make us feel a certain way. The problem with this is that we become like black holes, sucking in all that we desire and still wanting more.

God, the Creator of black holes, is the only one who can satisfy us. Pursuits are endless unless they end in Christ. When we find our satisfaction in Christ, we bring him glory, we find contentment, and it is in our best interest. Becoming a believer, however, doesn't flip a switch and make us satisfied. It's a continuous, working relationship of us seeking the Lord and him responding to our needs.

If you feel dissatisfied, don't be discouraged. Turn to the Lord and ask him to fill you again.

GRACEFULNESS

She is clothed with strength and dignity,
and she laughs without fear of the future.
When she speaks, her words are wise,
and she gives instructions with kindness.

PROVERBS 31:25-26 NLT

Scripture often uses clothing to relate to a person's spiritual state. We see this in Genesis, with Adam and Eve in the garden, all the way to the book of Revelation speaking about believers clothed in white for purity. Though the Proverbs 31 woman, described in the above verses, has fine linen clothing, it is not the outer garments that make her a good example, but the spiritual ones she wears. She clothes herself in strength of character and gracefulness of conduct.

These things are not reserved for women. Men should clothe themselves in these things, too, for these are fruits of the Spirit. The Proverbs 31 woman is full of grace because the fruit of the Holy Spirit is in her life. She is an example because the Holy Spirit is displaying his character in her life.

Show grace toward those around you by living your life in submission to the Holy Spirit and desiring for his fruits to grow in you.

WARMTH

There the angel of the LORD appeared to him in flames of fire from within a bush. Moses saw that though the bush was on fire it did not burn up.

EXODUS 3:2 NIV

Have you ever witnessed a natural phenomenon? It could be beautiful, like the northern lights, or a bit dangerous, like volcanic lightning. Did it engage you and if so, did you dare to get close to the spectacle, or did you keep your distance?

Moses encountered a miraculous event in the burning bush. Have you ever put yourself in his sandals and wondered how you would have reacted? Would the warmth of the fire invite you? Or would you run away from this strange bush that didn't burn? Whether curious or careless, Moses approached the blaze and met the angel of the Lord. This is when God revealed his calling on Moses's life. He would lead his chosen people out of Egypt and into the Promised Land.

Since Scripture says the Lord is the same yesterday, today and forever, keep your eyes open for a burning bush. All things are possible with God.

RIGHTEOUSNESS

The result of righteousness will be peace;
the effect of righteousness
will be quiet confidence forever.

Isaiah 32:17 CSB

The soothing sound of a waterfall, the warmth of the sun on a bright summer day, the laughter of a child, the coziness of a cup of tea and a good book on a winter's night, the security of having family and friends you can count on, the satisfaction of being told you have done a good job—all these things bring joy and a sense of peace, but the peace of God is the result of righteousness.

According to Scripture, the righteous delight in God's law and meditate on it day and night. They prosper in all the do, are morally excellent, and never listen to the advice of the wicked. Yet his Word also says there are none that are righteous, so how will we find peace? The answer is Jesus. When we place our faith in Christ, his righteousness becomes our righteousness because we are filled with his Spirit. Once we belong to Jesus, we are sealed, and nothing can come between us and the promises of our God.

Your salvation is sure and your eternity secure. No other truth brings more peace.

VALUE

Do not love the world or anything in the world. If anyone loves the world, love for the Father is not in them.

1 John 2:15 NIV

There is a way to watch media that is called bingeing. Streaming channels present multiple seasons of series at all once, enabling us to watch hour upon hour of one show in a sitting. Addicted to viewing television in this fashion, we brag about the fact that we finished a whole season in one night. We're obsessed, giving precious hours of life to something that really doesn't offer much benefit to our lives.

When we allow entertainment or objects to become our primary focus, we are allowing ourselves to get entrapped with things the world values. If we kept a schedule of how much time we spent on things that have no heavenly value, we would most likely shudder at the inequality. Doesn't this indicate what we consider important in our lives? Maybe this is why God reminds us not to love the world or what it values.

If you are committed to the Father with love and devotion, you will want to spend more time in his presence rather than with things that will one day be gone.

CUT THE STATIC

God will continually revitalize you, implanting within you the passion to do what pleases him.

PHILIPPIANS 2:13 TPT

There are two things we need to do if we are going to seek God's glory while chasing our dreams. First, live in faith. God loves faith. He rewards those who step out in faith and who trust in him. It pleases your Father in heaven when you have faith, and his pleasure never takes a downward spiral if you mess up while pursuing him.

Secondly, we need to practice self-control. Saying yes to God and stepping out in faith in one area will usually result in needing to say no to things that would get you off track. We must cut out the static of other things if we are going to wholeheartedly pursue our calling from God.

Ask God to show you what he has planned for you. Be ready to step out in faith.

FAITH-BUILDING WORDS

I would like to learn just one thing from you: Did you receive the Spirit by works of the law, or by believing what you heard?

GALATIANS 3:2 NIV

We cannot expect our faith to grow on its own. Jesus likened faith to a mustard seed, saying that if we have that much, it could move a mountain. Faith is like a seed in other ways, too. It grows in the soil of his love, under the nourishment of his Word. When we water it with testimonies of his goodness and with the truth of Jesus' life, then it will grow.

What can you listen to or read today to help build your faith? Start in God's Word, surely, but also remember the testimonies of others. Perhaps there is a book you have been wanting to read or a friend you have been meaning to catch up with. Stories have power to move us and to help us grow in empathy and in expectation.

Be built up by the faith of others who have experienced the faithfulness of God. Be encouraged with the truth of his love in action.

GIFT OF SALVATION

"I have been found by those who did not seek me;
I have shown myself to those who did not ask for me."
But of Israel he says, "All day long I have held out my hands
to a disobedient and contrary people."

ROMANS 10:20-21 ESV

Although Israel had been given countless prophesies, teaching, and signs, they refused to recognize Jesus as their Messiah. They continued to strive to achieve righteousness by upholding the law and failed to realize that Jesus Christ was the completion of the law: all of God's laws were in place to point to Christ.

So fixated were the people on the letter of the law that they overlooked its message of love. At the core of their unbelief, there existed an unwillingness to accept the truth. It is imperative that we humble ourselves to accept Christ's free and undeserved gift of salvation by the power of his Word.

Don't get caught up in attempting to achieve righteousness by your own merit. Listen to the words of God and accept his truth.

ONE WHO KNOWS

How can people call on him for help if they've not yet believed? And how can they believe in one they've not yet heard of? And how can they hear the message of life if there is no one there to proclaim it?

ROMANS 10:14 TPT

It's easy to forget the letters of the New Testament were letters to actual people in actual churches. When Paul wrote this to the Romans, he wasn't being figurative. He was explaining to them that they could believe the stories they were hearing.

The good news of a great healer who took on the sin of the world, all so they could be forgiven—was true. What the apostles preached, they heard straight from Jesus. What Paul wrote inspired faith, as it does to this day.

You can have faith in what you read in God's Word because it is truth. What you read is what he said, what he did, and what it all means.

BEING KNOWN

You know what I long for, LORD;
you hear my every sigh

PSALM 38:9 NLT

Think of the most perfect gift you've ever received. Not the most extravagant, but the one that was just so perfectly you that you realized the giver really knew you. They heard you, that one time, when you mentioned that one thing, perhaps in passing, and because they were listening with their heart, they saw into yours. They get you.

We love to be "gotten," and long to be seen. For many of us it's how we know we are loved. How much, then, must the Father love us? He who knows everything about us—who takes the time to listen to every longing and comfort every sigh—is waiting to give us his perfect gifts. We are known. We are loved.

Share your longing with God today. Let him show you his great love by revealing how intimately he knows you. Let him give you a good and perfect gift.

EYE ON YOU

In him we were also chosen, having been predestined according to the plan of him who works out everything in conformity with the purpose of his will, in order that we, who were the first to put our hope in Christ, might be for the praise of his glory.

EPHESIANS 1:11-12 NIV

Did you know that long before you decided to take the plunge and accept Christ into your heart as your Savior, he had his eye on you? He was waiting for you to come to him so that he could share with you his eternal gift. God wanted glorious living for you. And oh, how he celebrated when you made that decision!

It is through Christ that we discover who we are. When we put our hope in him, we find ourselves. It's in him that we learn what we are living for. And he works all of our lives together as Christians for the greater good.

You were chosen by God. He waited for you, and he rejoiced when you came to him. Celebrate with him today! Praise him for the gift he has given you in eternal salvation.

BEFORE BIRTH

You brought me out of the womb;
you made me trust in you,
even at my mother's breast.

PSALM 22:9 NIV

Jesus was the Word from the beginning—with God in the creation of this world and the creation of humanity. Jesus had a hand in creating you! It's great to know of Jesus as he was on earth, but it's also important to remember where and who he was from the beginning.

Jesus is a divine and human person, and he knows us so well. As we go into our days, we can be looking to recognize his Spirit speaking to us and working in us.

Jesus can not only empathize with you from a human perspective, but he also knows you inside out. Talk to him today as the person who knows you the best.

IN YOUR HAND

Let them praise the LORD,
because they were created by his command.

PSALM 148:5 NCV

God wants to use you in so many different ways, be it in your daily life or in a specific mission that he sets out for you. God doesn't, however, want you to try and be like somebody else in the way that you approach things. You don't have to talk like a famous preacher or lead a Bible study like your friend. You don't have to sing in the band to be influential.

God needs you to be you! He wants you to wear the things that make you who you are in order to do his work. David couldn't wear Saul's armor; he just needed his everyday attire to get the job done.

Wear your own shoes as you walk into today's tasks and be proud of them.

MAGNIFICENT

Yet what honor you have given to men,
created only a little lower than Elohim,
crowned with glory and magnificence.

PSALM 8:5 TPT

On the sixth day, after all other created things, God made man and woman. He made us in his image; this Scripture compares us to kings and queens! On that day he declared that his creation was very good.

How reassuring it is to know that God's creation was intentionally good. He did not create us with mistakes or flaws; he created us according to his perfect plan. As you wake up to a new day, consider how magnificent humanity is, and with that, how magnificent you are!

Thank God for his very good creation. Ask him to help you see beyond this life to the life to come where he will restore his creation to his perfect will.

A HEART TRUTH

"Do not look on his appearance or on the height of his stature, because I have rejected him. For the LORD sees not as man sees: man looks on the outward appearance, but the LORD looks on the heart."

1 SAMUEL 16:7 ESV

Every now and then, we are all surprised by the outcome of a situation. We think the dark horse will not win the race, or we underestimate the quiet contender vying for the workplace promotion. It is time to rest in the Lord and let him speak to us in his considerable wisdom.

God knows what he is doing. Perhaps your life has not turned out as you thought it should, and perhaps this has seemed for the better or for the worse. In either case, God sets in place those he wishes to use for his purposes. It is best to be a clean, yielded vessel and to chase after what drives you toward your best offering to Jesus.

Let God look at your heart and judge you beyond what your peers may see. He is always pleased with the humble heart that is rendering the fruit he desires.

BE PATIENT

Always be humble and gentle. Be patient with each other, making allowance for each other's faults because of your love.

EPHESIANS 4:2 NLT

Although we serve one God and share one faith, we are each created uniquely. Rather than reject and reprove the faults of others, we should use our strengths to help others in their weaknesses. In turn, other believers may help us when we are struggling.

The trademarks of a true Christian are clearly communicated here. We are to be humble, gentle, patient, and loving. Over and over Christ demonstrated these characteristics, even when it was not fair, convenient, or reciprocated. As his followers, we are called to live the same way. This is how the world will recognize who Christ really is.

Jesus chose to live humbly, yet his life impacted the entire world and still does to this day. With his testimony as your example, walk as he walked and choose the humble path as well.

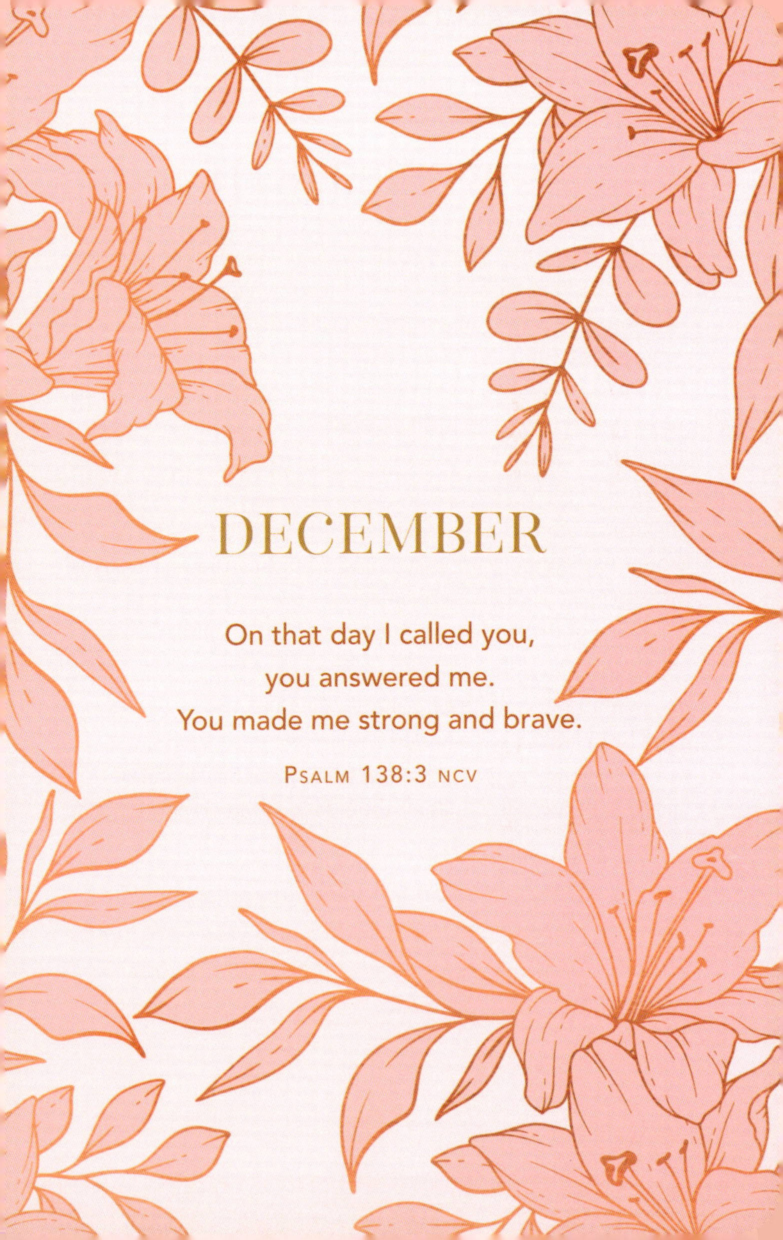

DECEMBER

On that day I called you,
you answered me.
You made me strong and brave.

Psalm 138:3 NCV

LAW AND FAITH

We ourselves are Jews by birth and not Gentile sinners; yet we know that a person is not justified by works of the law but through faith in Jesus Christ, so we also have believed in Christ Jesus, in order to be justified by faith in Christ and not by works of the law, because by works of the law no one will be justified.

GALATIANS 2:15-16 ESV

The Jews had to change their mindset that keeping the law brought salvation to understanding that just believing in Jesus was their justification. Sometimes we have to change our paradigm of thinking and behaving because of what Christ has done too.

You might be someone who checks all the boxes in your moral code book, which is a wonderful thing, yet there's a point where you have to realize that isn't where your salvation or faith merits come from. It's all about faith in the grace of Christ.

Get new perspective on the fact that you are justified because you believe in Jesus. Reserve your judgments about people and remember it is their belief, not actions, that save them too.

BUILT TOGETHER

Together, we are his house, built on the foundation of the apostles and the prophets. And the cornerstone is Christ Jesus himself.

EPHESIANS 2:20 NLT

While every home looks a little different, they all have foundations. As a believer, you have the same foundation of faith as your fellow Christians. This is an important thing to remember when faced with understandings and debates of different doctrines and practices. It does no good to the world when Christians begin to fight among themselves.

If you find yourself in battles with other believers, take a step back and remind yourself of what is common to you. Remember the teachings from Scriptures and recall that Jesus is the lens to apply in all of your thoughts.

Make every effort to unite yourselves with your brothers and sisters in faith.

FAITH AND WORKS

Just as the body without the spirit is dead, so also faith without works is dead.

JAMES 2:26 NASB

A body is no less a body when there isn't a spirit, but it doesn't truly represent who a person is unless they are breathing, moving, and speaking. In the same way, our faith is still faith, but it doesn't really represent Christ until it is moving and speaking.

There are times when you may have felt condemned because you haven't done enough with your faith. This kind of thinking is not from God. You don't earn your salvation through works; your salvation has already been gifted through Jesus.

Become a beautiful representation of Christ by choosing to give your faith life through your gracious actions and kind deeds.

ROOTED

Walk in Him, having been firmly rooted and now being built up in Him and established in your faith, just as you were instructed, and overflowing with gratitude.

COLOSSIANS 2:6-7 NASB

The windstorm was intense, destroying nearly everything in its path. Debris filled the streets as shingles blew off roofs. People ran for cover to avoid being hit by falling tree limbs. If not for basements, many might have sustained injuries. However, one tree in the middle of town was unaffected. Its owner had nurtured it from a sapling, carefully attending to its health. The roots had grown strong and sturdy, extending deep into the ground. No one yelled, "Timber!" for the old tree was solidly attached.

Jesus instructs us in his Word to stay connected to him. When we walk with him, commune with him, and grow stronger in our beliefs through faith, it helps us bear fruit in his name. In him, nothing is impossible for us. As we sit at his feet reading his Word, we mature in knowledge. We trust him with a faith that is unwavering because we understand his character, power, and great love for us.

Build your faith solidly on Jesus so you are not shaken in the storms.

NOT OF YOURSELF

By grace you have been saved through faith, and that not of yourselves; it is the gift of God.

Ephesians 2:8 NKJV

We tend to expect a lot of ourselves. There are so many things on our to do list. The house needs constant maintenance, meals need to be cooked, the finances need to be reorganized, not to mention our day Jobs! We work to get results and this can become part of our worldview when it comes to our faith.

Take some time to read this verse over and over. It is not about anything that you do, or try to do, that earns you salvation. You are loved and you are forgiven simply because you believe. Allow yourself to experience freedom from that truth and share the same kind of graciousness toward others.

Today, choose not to expect things from people; just freely give!

WORK OF FAITH

"Now I commit you to God and to the word of his grace, which is able to build you up and to give you an inheritance among all who are sanctified."

ACTS 20:32 CSB

Paul did incredible works for Christ. He preached, performed miracles, was put in prison, and was beaten for his faith. Paul held firm to his calling despite all the obstacles, and he learned to be content and joyful throughout the hardest times. His words to carry on this faith are encouraging.

You might feel like you have gone through a lot for your faith, whether it is people who don't believe you, or living a hard life where you still proclaim that God is good. Remember that today this message from hundreds of years ago is for you; it is a message of grace, a message able to build you up when you remember the inheritance you have in Christ.

Remember the inheritance you have in Jesus and be strengthened by his message of grace.

CLEAR VIEWS

Do not turn your back on me.
Do not reject your servant in anger.
You have always been my helper.
Don't leave me now; don't abandon me,
O God of my salvation!

PSALM 27:9 NLT

The psalmist petitioned God by acknowledging his character. He speaks of the God of his salvation, his only hope. These past experiences are how he relates to God. In many other places in the Bible we are called to be people who remember.

A person of remembrance recounts what God has done and acknowledges and praises him for it. This act of worship helps build faith during hard seasons. Let faith rise up in you. Remember a time when God was your salvation or your hope.

Pray a prayer of thanksgiving with this sweet memory and confidence in your God.

FIRM FOUNDATION

This is what the Sovereign LORD says: "Look! I am placing a foundation stone in Jerusalem, a firm and tested stone. It is a precious cornerstone that is safe to build on. Whoever believes need never be shaken."

ISAIAH 28:16 NLT

Architects know that for a building to stand, it must first have a good foundation. This means digging down to the bedrock and supporting the weight by laying strong footings. Only then can a successful structure be built. Your Christian life is like that tower. God laid the foundation when you gave your life to him. It is a strong foundation. Since that time, each bit of knowledge, every prayer, every verse has laid down the walls. When you obeyed the Word of God and showed his love to others, the walls took shape. Slowly they rose, strong on the cornerstone of your faith and held together by God.

You can take a brave stand in your relationships with others. Share what you know about the Lord and what he has done in your life. Don't be afraid of standing strong when the world mocks you. God stands with you. He is the firm foundation, ever mighty and carrying you through the perils of life. Don't be afraid. Stand strong.

Thank God for the foundational truths he has shared with you. Remember that he is always supporting you.

GREAT HUNTING

"Go therefore and make disciples of all nations, baptizing them in the name of the Father and of the Son and of the Holy Spirit, teaching them to observe all that I have commanded you. And behold, I am with you always, to the end of the age."

MATTHEW 28:19-20 ESV

There's a part of one farm that has always been kept for hunting. That's where the dove field, deer blind, and other hunting areas are, and Farmer Stu works hard to keep the fields ready for the hunters. Josh and Martin are brothers and they always hunt together. When turkey season opens, they are usually the first to ask if the fields are ready. Then the word gets out.

As believers we may not kill turkeys. But we do hunt for seekers and others who need to hear the gospel. Often once we begin talking about faith and the difference it makes in our lives, we find more than one person within earshot who is interested in hearing the gospel. At that moment, we realize we are on a hunt on God's behalf, looking to bring others into a relationship of faith in him.

Be mindful that there are people around you who need to hear about God's love.

RUN THE RACE

I know that I have not yet reached that goal, but there is one thing I always do. Forgetting the past and straining toward what is ahead.

Philippians 3:13 NCV

Paul confessed that he did not completely understand the full power of Christ's love and resurrection, but he stayed constant in his journey of following Jesus. He compared his faith walk to a race: training, straining, and pushing toward the prize at the end.

We are at times left exhausted, but the end goal is worth it all. Each of us is on a journey of sanctification, and there is grace for us. Just like a real race, looking back will distract us and slow us down, so we must not dwell on past mistakes. Our focus should be forward on what God is doing in our lives, and where he is leading us. God's grace is far greater than our mistakes, and our call is to leave the past behind while straining for what is ahead.

Make the goal of your entire life to serve God. He is your reward, your reason for racing, and the prize you cling to. He forgives the past and gives you a hopeful future.

BELIEVE IN THE SON

"God so loved the world that he gave his one and only Son, that whoever believes in him shall not perish but have eternal life. For God did not send his Son into the world to condemn the world, but to save the world through him."

JOHN 3:16-17 NIV

It is good to be reminded of the simple truth of the gospel. This verse is so popular because it sums up our faith so well. This was God's plan for the world and his plan for you.

God loved you so much that he gave his Son, Jesus. When you believe in him, you have eternal life. It's a great thought to take into your day. Let the hope of eternal life give you the perspective you need to face today's challenges. You are no longer condemned to death; you are saved.

Be reminded of God's amazing grace today.

A BLAZING FURNACE

Shadrach, Meshach and Abednego replied to him, "King Nebuchadnezzar, we do not need to defend ourselves before you in this matter. If we are thrown into the blazing furnace, the God we serve is able to deliver us from it, and he will deliver us from Your Majesty's hand."

DANIEL 3:16-17 NIV

Wouldn't it be incredible to have such unwavering faith? These three men were so convinced that God would save them from the fire that they didn't even try to plead their case before the king.

You are unlikely to face a literal fiery furnace, but when you are challenged about your faith, think of this situation and remember to stand up for what you believe and who you believe in. God is the only God who truly saves. He finds ways to show his power and reality in big and small ways.

Look for opportunities to declare your faith to others today.

HEAVENLY CITIZENSHIP

Our citizenship is in heaven, from which we also eagerly wait for the Savior, the Lord Jesus Christ.

PHILIPPIANS 3:20 NKJV

An aspect of our lives that citizenship affects is that sometimes we will be asked to lay down our rights. If you are a citizen of a free country, this can be especially hard. We think it is our right to punish our enemies, to have wealth, to be able to say whatever we want. While these aren't strictly bad things, they are things the Bible says we will need to lay down. You can probably think of other examples that are more personal to you.

Why do we assume we have the right to religious freedom? The early church did not, and they flourished. Why do we assume that we can kill our enemies? Doesn't Jesus tell us to love them? Making yourself first a citizen in the kingdom can turn your life upside down as you begin to live by kingdom principles.

Live on earth as a citizen of heaven. Let Jesus guide you on the journey, for he will be the one to welcome you home.

DIRECTED PATHS

In all your ways acknowledge Him,
and He shall direct your paths.

PROVERBS 3:6 NKJV

God watches over us, cares for us, and is involved in our lives. When we acknowledge that every good thing comes from him, our faith is strengthened, and we are able to trust him more.

God has been involved in everything that has gone on today. He is a constant presence in your decisions and conversations. He is with you in the good and difficult times, and you can continue to trust him to lead the way.

Make a point of noticing how God has directed your path today, and thank him for being trustworthy. Acknowledge that his goodness in your life will lead you in the right way.

PLAY WELL

Sing to Him a new song;
Play skillfully with a shout of joy.

Psalm 33:3 NKJV

The clean slate of a new day is filled with an air of expectation. It's like deep down inside there is something built into our heart and mind that longs to start afresh. This morning is the chance for you to start again. You may have had a bad day yesterday or felt like you didn't complete what you needed to, but today is a new and different day!

Whether you are a goal setter or someone who approaches the day with a whatever-may-come attitude, you have God's mercy and grace to help you achieve it.

Thank God for letting you start new today and every day. Pray for faith to see what he has already begun doing.

TRULY KNOWN

Keep a good conscience so that in the thing in which you are slandered, those who disparage your good behavior in Christ will be put to shame.

1 Peter 3:16 NASB

A conversation filters through the grapevine and makes its way to you. Someone made a derogative comment about your character or a statement about you that was an outright lie. It's a shock, and it stings. How should you react?

When you are confident in who you are in Christ and how your life reflects him, you don't need to react. You simply need to remember and reflect that you know the truth, and so does the one who matters most—Jesus. He knows your heart and your desire to live as he did.

Rejoice in knowing that you are fully and truly known.

MEASURING STICKS

Do you not realize this about yourselves,
that Jesus Christ is in you?

2 Corinthians 13:5 ESV

Many of us go through life trying to measure up. It could be put on by our parents, teachers, coaches, friends, or even ourselves, but at some point we all grab a hold of a measuring stick and try to see what we are worth. Sometimes we exceed the standards. Other times we use the sticks to flog ourselves, beating ourselves up with shame when we don't measure up.

You might even see the Bible as a measuring stick: an impossible standard of God that you will never live up to. That is true; on our own we could never measure up to God's holiness. But the good news is, in Christ, we do. When God looks at you, he sees Christ's righteousness which measures up completely. You are good enough because of Jesus. You achieve things because of Jesus.

Jesus has met the goal and exceeded the standards, so you don't need to try to be perfect anymore. Praise God for this freedom in him!

WHO HE IS

In Your great mercy You did not utterly consume them
nor forsake them;
For You are God, gracious and merciful.

NEHEMIAH 9:31 NKJV

"That's just how she is." Have you ever heard someone say this about someone else? It's a conclusive statement, lacking in faith that the person will ever change if referring to a negative characteristic or full of wonder if it's positive. It's as though we could sum up a person's entire personality and life with a short description. While it might not be best when describing someone else, it's awesome when describing God. Who is God? He's always gracious and merciful; that's just who he is!

When we sum someone up with one comment to someone else, that person tends to then only see that characteristic in the person. It's like when you are shopping for a car and you hope to buy a certain type, suddenly you see that same car everywhere. You notice it; they stand out. Nehemiah is describing God and what stands out about him in this passage. He uses the words gracious and merciful. That's just who he is! Praise him for this today.

How do you sum up God? How do you think others sum you up? Ask yourself if you reflect the character of God.

FOR SENSITIVE SOULS

Be kind to each other, tenderhearted, forgiving one another, just as God through Christ has forgiven you.

EPHESIANS 4:32 NLT

Maybe you view your sensitivity as a weakness. The question is, who made you that way? God did! He made you in his image. He gave you these gifts. Does that make God weak? Certainly not! We serve a compassionate, feeling God who is far from weak. He gave you these gifts because he knows our body of believers needs them to be strong.

So, put on your compassion. Speak out of kindness. Serve in humility. You are beloved by God, and you are needed in the body of Christ. Don't shrink away from feeling all the feelings he has given you. Love deeply, knowing that your heavenly Father is proud of you.

Jesus cares for you deeply. He can show you how to use your gifts to care for others.

ALREADY QUALIFIED

Not that we are competent in ourselves to claim anything for ourselves, but our competence comes from God.

2 Corinthians 3:5 NIV

There is nothing we can do to qualify ourselves for grace. You also need no qualifications to be God's instrument. You don't need to go to Bible school. You don't need to be a pastor. You don't need to memorize a whole book of the Bible or wear your hair a certain way. You don't need to be old and experienced.

God wants to use you, dear believer of God! He has chosen this time in history, this place on the globe, and your unique talents and gifts, all for his glory. You are qualified to serve because you are in Christ.

Don't let anyone tell you otherwise. Walk in the boldness of your calling today!

CONSIDER IT

When I consider Your heavens, the work of Your fingers,
the moon and the stars, which you have ordained,
what is man that You are mindful of him,
and the son of man that You visit him?

Psalm 8:3-4 NKJV

When we look at nature and all the intricacies of creation, there is so much beauty in the design. There are galaxies we don't know a thing about, species in the depths of the sea that have not yet been discovered. There is so much that we do not know, and there is beauty all around.

The Creator of all things is also the one who made us. He knit us together with intention. He knows us better than we know ourselves. He sees us as a whole and knows us each intimately. He is aware of the number of hairs on our heads. He knows the songs that get us out of our seats. He knows.

Be drawn to his love today through the awe and wonder of his attention to detail. He does not miss a thing.

RIGHTFUL PURSUIT

The one who pursues righteousness and faithful love will find life, righteousness, and honor.

Proverbs 21:21 CSB

God is light, and in him everything is brought to light. He makes the most muddled situations clear with the precision of his perspective. As we pursue God's good nature in our lives, we will find the life and honor we are looking for. We will find all the fullness we seek in the virtues of our God and King.

As we worship God, we begin to understand that he is better than any expression of love we encounter on this earth. He is purer than our highest morals. He has no hidden motives, and as we are filled by his revelation light, we find that we need not.

Your loving response to living submitted to God's heart is a natural response to the unfiltered worth you find in being loved by the King of kings.

GUARDED BY WISDOM

Wisdom will enter your heart,
and knowledge will fill you with joy.

PROVERBS 2:10 NLT

Wisdom is not a vain pursuit. We may spend our time increasing our knowledge in various ways, but true wisdom is found in God. In his Word, we find keys to living in the light of wisdom. A good starting place is to look at the life of Jesus. He is wisdom embodied.

Where in life do you need understanding? Human insight only goes so far. Will you lean into the Lord and ask for his perception over your circumstances? He has the answers and solutions for each problem that arises. You can trust him to guide you through every difficulty.

God can guide you through the maze of your circumstances. If you are at a loss, ask for his wisdom. He will breathe revelation light into your mind and let you see from his perspective.

ALL COME TRUE

Mary responded, "I am the Lord's servant. May everything you have said about me come true." And then the angel left her.

LUKE 1:38 NLT

Given the extraordinary news that she, an unwed teenager, would bear the Son of God, Mary agreed without hesitation. "I am the Lord's servant." Can you imagine? No questions, no doubts, and no fears, just humble acceptance. Look at what she says next: "May everything you have said about me come true." What beautiful faith, what trust!

What do you suppose the Lord has spoken over you and your life? Given his abiding love for you, it can only be something wonderful. Despite our limited understanding of his ways, we can trust—with the certainty of Mary—that anything the Lord speaks over our lives is the only truth we need to fulfill.

Be empowered and emboldened to explore every desire God has placed in your heart, and to develop and use every talent you have been given for the glory of his kingdom.

JOURNEY OF FAITH

When they saw the star, they rejoiced exceedingly with great joy.

MATTHEW 2:10 ESV

There are some extremely descriptive words here. *Rejoiced exceedingly* with *great joy*? We know without a doubt how the wise men reacted! They had spent their whole lives studying the stars. Imagine the patience and diligence that took. Then, they found a new star and left their homelands, traveling miles and miles, believing the star would lead them where they wanted to go. When the star finally stopped, they believed that they were in the place of the new king. What faith!

God has a calling for your life, and he may be asking you to step out in faith and follow him. Then, when the journey is done, he might ask for even more belief from you. Perhaps the destination doesn't look like you thought. Did the magi expect a humble house and a poor child? God wants you to trust him all the same.

Prepare, have faith, and believe.

ON THE HORIZON

You have been united with Christ Jesus. Once you were far away from God, but now you have been brought near to him through the blood of Christ.

Ephesians 2:13 NLT

Have you ever seen a black speck on the horizon of the ocean, realizing it is a vessel but not sure exactly what type or how large it is? It seems like it is something spectacular, but you can't make out any of the features or understand what its purpose is until it gets nearer.

Jesus Christ brought God's plan for humanity close to us so now when we look at him, we understand the detail and beauty of what God has done for us. We were far away from the truth, but now it has been brought close.

Thank God for helping you see things clearly when you didn't understand or know quite what salvation meant. Ask him to help you bring that vessel closer to others today so they may experience his nearness as well.

YOU ARE PERFECT

By a single offering he has perfected for all time those who are being sanctified.

HEBREWS 10:14 ESV

Stop, go back, and read that again. You are perfect. Looking in the mirror, or thinking back over your week, it is easy to forget or disbelieve those words. Don't let that happen. A wrinkle here, a bulge there, an unkind word, or a jealous thought cannot change the way the Father sees you. And it's how he wants you to see yourself.

The dictionary uses 258 words to explain what it means to be perfect, but we only need to know this: We are complete. When he chose to die on the cross for our sins, Jesus took away every flaw from those of us who love him. He finished what we never could; he made us perfect.

If possible, go to the mirror you see yourself in most often. Stand before it and ask God to show you what he sees when he looks at you. See past the flaws, past any hurt or anger in your eyes, past any perceived imperfection. See yourself complete, just as you were meant to be. See yourself perfect

SPIRITUAL HERITAGE

The LORD set his affection on your ancestors and loved them, and he chose you, their descendants, above all the nations—as it is today.

DEUTERONOMY 10:15 NIV

Genealogies are very popular. There are companies who sell DNA kits that can tell you who your ancestors were and various other aspects of your biological history, all from a swab of the inside of your cheek. The fascination of finding out who we are and where we came from has made these companies quite successful.

These genetic tests cannot tell you if your ancestors were believers in Christ or not, but the Old Testament has many true stories about your spiritual ancestors. There are accounts in the Word that reveal God's promise to patriarchs Abraham, Isaac, and Jacob about how their descendants would be unnumberable. His Word contains your spiritual heritage.

You can be certain that, even if you don't know your ancestors' beliefs, you are the chosen of God, and you are sealed in him through Christ.

RECOGNIZE

When he was at the table with them, he took the bread and blessed it and broke it and gave it to them. And their eyes were opened, and they recognized him. And he vanished from their sight. They said to each other, "Did not our hearts burn within us while he talked to us on the road, while he opened to us the Scriptures?"

Luke 24:30-32 ESV

If you read the entirety of Luke 24, you find that today's verse is from the story of two travelers walking down the road after the resurrection of Jesus. Jesus comes up beside them and essentially plays dumb, asking them what had happened. The account says they did not recognize him. He then explains to them, using all of Scripture, the truth about himself. When the time was right, at the supper table over the bread, he allowed their eyes to be opened.

Many have questioned why Jesus chose to blind their eyes to who he was at first. Though we don't have an answer to that question, there is no doubt that their spirits recognized Jesus. It says that their hearts burned with them at hearing the good news. Have you had this experience? Has your heart burned with passionate love because of the Holy Spirit working in your heart?

God is real! Recognize his presence and praise him for it.

LABELS

Stop dwelling on the past.
Don't even remember these former things.
I am doing something brand new, something unheard of.

Isaiah 43:18-19 TPT

From a young age, people like to label other people. We put each other in groups at school: the cool kids, the band kids, the goth kids, and so on. We don't let go of this labeling obsession once we leave high school. Even as adults, we like to fit others into neat categorical boxes. Maybe some of these labels you impose on yourself. Perhaps they make you feel safe, or they are what you have been told your whole life. It might be pretty, plain, talented, rebellious, a bother, athletic, smart, nerdy, and on and on.

Perhaps it is time we shake off all these labels that we let define us and take on just one—in Christ. The Bible has a lot to say about who you are in Christ. You are chosen, loved, a child of God, a friend of God, justified, and this wonderful list goes on.

Don't let labels, good or bad, be the shaping factor in your life. Accept your identity in Christ and let your status as new creation reign.

GROW SPIRITUALLY

Grow in the grace and knowledge of our Lord and Savior Jesus Christ. To him be glory both now and forever! Amen.

2 PETER 3:18 NIV

The end of the year is a time of reflection. It gives most of us the urge to look back over the year that has passed. As you look back, did you grow spiritually? Your walk with Christ is the most important relationship and aspect of your life. Your life should be centered around Christ and bringing him glory; it's the purpose of every human being. With this in mind, how did you see growth in your relationship this year?

The point is not to look for perfection. None of us will be perfect this side of heaven. It is also not to measure how many good works you did to see if you qualify for salvation. No, the point is to take an honest look at the state of your heart. Are your life choices helping you to grow in Christ, or are you wilting?

Make your time, priorities, and lifestyle reflect growth and give glory to God.